Mortgages, Money, and Life

52 Lessons on a New Way of Looking at Owning a Home, Creating Wealth, and Making Smarter Decisions with Your Money

Trevor Hammond

Mortgages, Money, and Life

Printed by:
90-Minute Books
302 Martinique Drive
Winter Haven, FL 33884
www.90minutebooks.com

Published in the United States of America

170202-00694-2

ISBN-13: 978-1643200125
ISBN-10: 1643200127

For more information on 90-Minute Books including finding out how you
can publish your own book, visit 90minutebooks.com or call (863) 318-0464

Here's What's Inside...

Foreword

First, why the title?

Not long ago, someone was asking me about my business. This person was asking what made me and my team so unique in the world of residential mortgage and what I attributed my success to.

Without thinking, I answered, "People come to us looking for a mortgage. As quickly as I can, I get them to realize the mortgage discussion is really about money. And most money decisions, plans and goals come down to what you want your life to look like."

By helping people first get clear on their money goals and life goals, the mortgage planning and implementation on how to handle their real estate financing took on an entirely new importance.

Second, how should you read this book?

This book is a compilation of 52 mini-lessons on mortgages, money, and life. Some are thought-provoking, and others are more tactical habits and strategies.

I have put the lessons in the order I feel we should approach everything, starting with life, then moving to money, and then finishing with strategies on how best to handle your mortgage borrowing and repayment strategies.

I understand that very few people around the world read non-fiction books. Even those that start a book fight the odds of actually finishing a book. Knowing this to be true, here is my advice to you to get the most out of this book. **Read one lesson per week.** Each lesson should take less than five minutes. Even if you have more time, do NOT read the next one until next week. Instead, take the time to think about the lesson and how it might be applied in your life. Some lessons might be simple ways to expand your thinking, while other lessons might take you some quiet time somewhere away from the noise and chaos of your normal life to do some serious planning.

Finally, have fun with it! Grab a beer or a glass of wine, or a hot cup of green tea or coffee, and enjoy a few minutes to read. And as you do, remind yourself it's the only life you have, so what you do with it is kind of important. If you aren't "feeling" some of the lessons, that's ok. If you don't agree with something, that's ok too...that's why it's MY book. (Insert smiley face emoji with tongue sticking out).

I've always loved to coach others. From coaching my younger brothers in basketball in my youth, to now coaching my children's soccer teams, I have always loved seeing the kids learn and grow and have fun along the way. In my professional life, I have come to realize my passion for coaching simply takes on a different form – coaching homeowners and home buyers how to make the smartest financial decisions to help them achieve a bigger, better, safer financial future.

Third, WHY did I write this book? More importantly...why should you care?

Don't get me wrong...it's really all about you. This book is for you, and all about you. You are the hero of your story. How you interpret the lessons here will be unique to you, where you are in life, and where you hope to be someday.

The reason this book is now in your hands is that I am on the same journey as you! I have been studying and practicing ways to enjoy more money, less stress, and more life for many years now. I've had good years and bad years. Along the way, I have learned that there is only *'winning and learning'*. So, this book is simply a way for me to share what has worked for me on my personal journey. The hope is that the lessons in the following pages will make your path on this same journey just a bit easier, or perhaps faster and safer.

I learned long ago that I can't help everyone I would like to. I only have so many hours in a day, week, or year to personally sit with people and coach them through a new way of thinking, planning, and executing their money habits when it comes to owning and financing real estate. I needed to multiply my efforts, so I could impact the most people in the shortest amount of time. My hope is that even one of the lessons in this book influences you to think differently or moves you in a new direction, so you can ***enjoy more money, less stress, and a better life***.

Life

#1 - Planning Your Best Year Ever – Begin With the End in Mind

We've all heard the sound wisdom of Stephen Covey, author of *The 7 Habits of Highly Effective People*, "Begin with the end in mind." As you eagerly look ahead to the New Year, I want you to take a different approach this time around to ensure you make it your best year ever!

Let's fast forward to the *end* of the upcoming year. Imagine yourself alone in your favorite thinking spot, reflecting *back* over the previous year. Now answer this question:

Looking back over the previous twelve months, what HAS to have happened for you to be happy with your progress this past year?

The difference here is, rather than writing down goals you *hope* to achieve in the year ahead, you are transporting yourself a year into the future and looking back, so you now may describe the year as if it's about to come to a close. Write down things you have accomplished or made progress on in past tense, as if it's already happened.

Here are some thinking questions to get you started:

- What did you accomplish this year that you are most proud of?
- What personal goals did you achieve?

- What business or professional goals did you accomplish?
- How much time did you commit to your growth? Your health? Your family and friends?
- What impact did you make on the lives of others?

With everything you write, be as specific as possible. For example, don't write down a goal "growing your business" or "losing weight". Instead, include ways of measuring your goal and write it in past tense such as, *"I increased revenue 10%"*, and *"I lost 15 pounds by eating healthier and exercising 3x per week."*

This may be tricky at first, but you will get better and better at it with practice. Know that the mind struggles when trying to accomplish things it deems impossible or two far-fetched. So, when we set big, grandiose goals that we aren't 100% confident we can achieve, our mind struggles. But by describing things in past tense, as if you've already accomplished them, you begin to trick your mind into seeing your goals as realistic and achievable.

#2 - Make Your Future Bigger and Better

When you think about your future, are you excited? Be honest with yourself. How "bright" do you feel your future is? How confident are you that your future will be better than your past?

I have found that confidence is the key to just about everything, and without it, life can be much more difficult. This can be especially true when envisioning an exciting, bright future.

Here is a fundamental philosophy I want you to think about and begin to implement into your life:

"Always imagine your future bigger and better than your past."

We all know people who subconsciously feel their past is better than anything coming in their future. These are the people who spend countless hours talking about their past accomplishments, or how thin they used to be, or even how much money they used to make. And yes, as you read this, you might catch yourself thinking..."wait, this is how I talk!"

We have to **make** our future bigger and better than our past. It doesn't happen by itself. It is a mindset. A bigger, better future can mean different things to different people. Perhaps you envision more money as the key to a better future, or being healthier and feeling better. Maybe a bigger, better future for you means feeling less "busy-ness" in your schedule and the freedom to spend more time on things you love doing and with the people you enjoy being around.

To get started on making your future bigger and better, ask yourself this question:

Imagine it is one year from now and you are reflecting on the past twelve months. What must have happened over the past year for me to be happy?

Be as specific as you can. Think about your relationships, your career, your health, your finances, and so on. Paint the picture as clear as possible. This will become your road map for a bigger, better future.

#3 - What Must You Become?

It's never just about achieving your goals. It's about what you become while pursuing your goals.

So often we set our sights on things we want, or goals we would like to achieve. We want a company to hire us, or our spouse to love us, or our children to cherish us. We want a raise or a promotion. And all too often, the results fail to match up with our expectations.

What if, instead of "chasing" these various goals and desires, we asked ourselves a question?

What must I become to attract _____?

Think about it. What must I become to make that company do whatever it takes to get me on board? What must I become for my spouse to wait with anticipation for me to come home?

What must I become for my children to choose time with me even over their friends? What must I become to get that promotion or win that business?

If you begin asking this question, you will begin to feel empowered. We cannot control the decisions other people make. Nor can we live our lives expecting them to always know how to please us or meet our needs. This way of thinking will lead to a life of frustration and disappointment.

Instead, look in the mirror and answer the question, "What must I become?"

#4 - Set Bigger Goals

One of the biggest mistakes we can make throughout our life is setting small goals. Oh, I understand why most people avoid setting bigger goals. It usually is due to a lack of confidence and probably a lack of skills or knowledge on how to achieve anything other than the small, incremental goals they write down. As the saying goes, be careful about setting goals too small...you just might achieve them. The other advice to keep at the forefront is this: there are no losers, only learners.

To get started, I will share one of the greatest secrets that helped me achieve incredible results, both personally and professionally. Commit first. Set a goal, and fully commit to it. Be all in. Only then will you have the courage to figure out the "how" and put in the work to achieve it. Achieving new goals, especially larger ones, usually requires learning new skills, creating new habits, or improving ourselves in some way so that we can achieve something we don't already have. Sometimes it can even mean surrounding yourself with different people.

As you look ahead, practice setting goals that excite you. Even more important, make those goals ones that excite those around you, such as your spouse, your children, or your employees and teammates.

Here are the top three reasons you must set bigger and bigger goals:

1. **Small goals don't excite you.** Small goals are boring. Small goals don't get you excited. Small, incremental goals don't cause you to wake up early in anticipation of the pursuit of something so exciting and motivating you won't be swayed! Small goals don't force you to make the big changes in your life that will dramatically IMPROVE your life. Small goes don't make your palms start sweating when you tell others what you are attempting to achieve. To make a significant change, you must set goals that scare you and keep you motivated for the long haul.

2. **Big goals will excite those around you.** Everyone wants to be a part of something special, and small, incremental goals are not special. They are safe but boring. They don't stretch anyone's capabilities. If done right, your goals can excite and motivate those around you. Your spouse will be excited. Your kids will be behind you holding you accountable. People at work will continuously check in on your progress. All of this will push you and keep you motivated.

If telling others causes too much stress for you, keep in mind it isn't as simple as just throwing out a big goal to those around you. Before sharing with anyone, take the time to map out a good plan on how you will actually achieve your goal. If the achievement of my goal might impact those I'm sharing it with, be sure to let them know! If you have tied a reward for achieving a certain goal, share that too. If your goal is to lose weight, don't just share how many pounds you want to shed. Share how you're changing your diet, as well as how often you will be using your lunch break to walk or run every day. Share how you will be adjusting your shopping habits, and having your kids get involved with eating healthier too. With all of this, you'll show you aren't just dreaming...you've got a plan, and are committed to making it happen!

3. **It's about what you become while pursuing big goals.** The biggest shift you will enjoy is in understanding what a big impact setting big goals will have on you and how you approach life. Setting bigger goals forces you to learn new capabilities. There is no longer any room in the future for your bad habits. As you work toward losing 50 pounds, you may find yourself a happier person. You might find your

relationship with your kids or spouse improves because you have more energy to engage in more activities. Instead of setting a goal to run a 5k, you instead set a goal to run a marathon...and along the way you meet new people with similar goals, lose more weight, watch less television, etc. It's exciting to not always know what other positive changes will come along the way of pursuing a big goal.

By setting goals that are so big and exciting, while having no idea YET how you'll achieve them, you begin your own journey toward massive, personal growth. Yes, you will fall on your face at times. You will make mistakes along the way. You will miss achieving some of your goals, but you will learn to appreciate the progress you made overall. Set big goals. Commit fully to them. And you just might achieve them.

#5 - 5 Things to Reflect On Today to Increase Your Confidence Tomorrow

Too often it seems we find ourselves focusing our attention on things that did not work, and all that we did not accomplish or get done that we had hoped. By focusing on the negative, over time this can actually drag down your confidence whether you realize it or not!

Why is having personal confidence so important?

Maintaining a high level of personal confidence (I did not say arrogance!) helps us overcome obstacles and setbacks that are placed in the way of achieving our goals. And when we break through barriers, we achieve personal growth!

Looking back over the last 90 days, here are five areas of your life to reflect on the progress you have made. Grab a piece of paper and list everything you can think of, big or small, that you have accomplished:

1. Progress with your family:
2. Progress with your health:
3. Progress with your work/career:
4. Progress with your finances:
5. Progress with your spiritual life:

Once you have your list, review it. Be proud of it. Hang it on a wall. Share it with others.

Throughout our days, weeks and months, we forget to celebrate our progress as we continuously pursue and expect "perfection". Chasing perfection is like chasing the horizon.

Since there is no "perfection", you can see how detrimental chasing this fantasy can be, leading us to never be satisfied and continuously frustrated. Our confidence in ourselves and our capabilities wanes. We fret over the seven items not crossed off on our daily to-do list, rather than patting ourselves on the back for the three items we completed!

Instead, make it a new habit to reflect daily or weekly on what you DID accomplish! Share it at the dinner table. Instill this habit in your children. When a friend or colleague is complaining about all they didn't get done that day, quickly change their perspective and ask them, "What DID you accomplish today?" Ask them, "What was your biggest WIN of the day?" Or you might inquire, "Where did you make progress today?" Be prepared for a surprised look, and then a growing sense of confidence, all thanks to you!

#6 - Boost Your Confidence - It Means Everything

One of the biggest breakthroughs I have personally had in recent years is realizing how important confidence is. I have come to believe that confidence is the key to just about everything, both personally and professionally.

In sales, the confident professional makes the calls, sets the meetings, and gets the business. In life, the confident person is cultivating relationships, making friends, helping others, and being a great parent. The confident child is doing well in class, being a good friend to others, and eager for the next challenge.

So if confidence truly is this important, how can we increase our own confidence? The simplest way I have learned is this:

Measure yourself by how far you've come, not by how far you still have to go.

This means creating a habit of constantly acknowledging the small accomplishments (progress) you make along the path to your ultimate goal. While most people are trained to not celebrate until (and if) they accomplish their goal, I have learned how important it is to celebrate your progress along the way.

Unfortunately, too many people don't take the time to acknowledge the small bits of progress they make along the way. Take for example a good friend of mine who is looking to lose weight. They have a goal of losing 25 pounds by the end of the year. So should they not celebrate their progress along the way and just wait until they hit the final goal? No! Maintaining the momentum is critical and it takes confidence to do so. This means they must celebrate along the way, as they knock off the first five pounds, or accomplish two weeks with no desserts. These are small victories on the path to the ultimate goal! If, on the other hand, they constantly base their progress on that one ideal result (25 pounds) then they will become increasingly frustrated and might lose momentum if it seems too far away.

Here is the new, better way to do this. Set the goal (lose 25 pounds by year-end, or have $10,000 in savings, etc.). Then, only measure yourself by "turning around" and measuring your progress based on where you were last week or last month. This alone will transform how you feel and increase your confidence dramatically!

Here are some other common examples I see all too often. Think about how you approach these or similar scenarios in your life.

- Your child takes third place in a competition. Her heart (and yours most likely) were set on getting first. But last year, she and the team didn't even place at all. What do you focus on? The fact she didn't get first? Or the amount of progress made since last year?

- You set a goal to have all of your consumer debt paid off this year, about $10,000. At the end of the year, you've paid off all but $2,200. You fell short due to an appliance needing to be replaced. What do you focus on? The fact you didn't get to $0 as planned or the fact you have $7,800 LESS DEBT now than a year ago?

- You and your spouse make a commitment to have two date nights per month. That's 24 over the course of the year or twelve half way through the year. So far you count only six actual date nights out without the kids due to unforeseen events. What do you focus on? The previous year you had no date nights out for just the two of you, or you're far behind on the goal you set for this year?

A small shift in what you focus on can change your life and take your confidence (and happiness) to new levels you never knew possible.

It's not easy changing the way you think. But it is very possible if you commit to it, and the reward is worth it.

#7 - Constant and Never-Ending Improvement (CANI)

Coaching expert, and author Tony Robbins coined this phrase (pronounced Kuhn-EYE) after the Japanese word "Kaizen", which means "constant improvement". *"...in order to succeed and be happy, we've got to be constantly improving the quality of our lives, constantly growing and expanding." – Tony Robbins, Awaken the Giant Within.*

Too often, we set big goals, only to disappoint ourselves when we do not accomplish them. We might say, "We will have an emergency fund with $10,000 in it by the end of the year!" But without a specific daily, weekly, and monthly plan to build towards this, the goal of saving $10,000 will not happen.

Understanding CANI, you can begin breaking this large goal down into bite-sized manageable steps. $10,000 over twelve months equates to $833 per month. This may still sound overwhelming to many.

What if you broke it down to an even smaller number, say $10,000 over 365 days? That is $28 per day. Suddenly a small, daily accomplishment of $28 saved per day seems manageable. At the same time, it still leads to our big goal of having a $10,000 "cash-cushion" at the end of one year.

Apply this principal to all aspects of your finances and life. Create a plan for constant and never-ending improvement for yourself!

- Rather than kid yourself that you will devote four hours each weekend to reading, or spending time with your kids, or exercising, block out 30 minutes each morning or night.
- Rather than waiting until Sunday dinner with the family to reflect on the previous week, finish each day by writing down three accomplishments, or "wins" you had that day.
- Choose a different night each week to review your spending habits with your spouse.

We can't always guarantee the ideal outcomes we desire, but we CAN control our activities and efforts that drive us in the right direction. Make a commitment to yourself to be proactive in achieving success with your money. Get passionate about creating more balance and fun in your life. We understand that money is the root of the stress for many families. It's up to you to take action to reduce (and remove) that stress.

#8 - Get Emotional About Your Goals

"People over-estimate what they can accomplish in one year, but underestimate what they can accomplish in a decade." – Anthony Robbins

The time is here! What big goals do you have this year? What were your big goals for last year? Did you achieve them? Why or why not?

If you are like millions of others, every year brings about excitement and a feeling of opportunity, as you say to yourself, "This year I really am going to _____!" Unfortunately, the excitement of achieving these goals quickly fizzles. Goals we thought were important to us apparently weren't important enough for us to make different choices each day and change our habits and behaviors necessary for success.

Why do most goals fail? We do not get emotional enough about them! Simply put, we don't dig deep enough on WHY a particular goal is really important to us. We stop short in connecting the specific goal to a bigger purpose in our life. Without this, all the planning and temporary excitement is a waste of time.

The 5 Why's – How to Emotionally Connect With Your Goals

This simple exercise can change your life. At a minimum, it will filter out unimportant goals and help you achieve the most important ones.

First, have your list of goals handy. Taking one goal at a time, start by asking yourself:

Why is achieving this goal important?

Once you have an answer, ask the same "why" question again with regards to your answer. Repeat this 5 times. At the end of the "5 Why's", you will find a much more important, compelling, and even emotional reason for truly wanting to accomplish this goal.

Let's walk through an example of losing weight. Imagine your goal is to lose 20 pounds this year: (sample answers are in parenthesis)

1. Why is losing 20 pounds important? *(To look and feel better!)*
2. Why is looking and feeling better important? *(So I have more energy during the day!)*
3. Why is having more energy during the day important? *(I want to have energy when I get home from work to play with the kids and not be so grumpy and tired!)*
4. Why is having the energy to play with your kids without being grumpy and tired important? *(Because I don't want them to look back on their childhood and not have good memories of time with me!)*
5. Why is it important that your kids have good childhood memories of spending time with you? *(So that when they grow up I don't have regrets and they still enjoy*

coming to visit and I get to spend time with my grandchildren someday!)

The question may seem redundant initially, and the answers obvious. But the true power is in connecting your goal to a bigger purpose in life that you will be emotionally connected to. In this example, we went from "looking and feeling better" to "not having regrets about our time with our children and fostering a future relationship with grandchildren". After the fifth "Why" question, you get to a powerful and emotional reason WHY you must do whatever it takes to lose that 20 pounds. Failure is not an option!

Without goals, you are simply getting through your day, rather than getting from the day.

Go back to your list of goals and apply the 5 Why's to each one. Filter out those you no longer feel emotionally attached to, and prioritize those that you do. Through simplicity comes clarity.

#9 - 3 Strategies to Create a Habit of Gratitude

Being truly grateful for things in our life can have a very positive impact on our relationships, career, marriage, emotional health, and more. And practicing gratitude is known to increase confidence since it is impossible to experience a negative emotion while you're being grateful for something.

Make it your goal to be grateful for the things you have every day, all year long. Too many of us practice gratitude sparingly, or only around the holidays. Being thankful for things your life, big and small, obvious and subtle, must become a daily habit.

Here are three unique strategies to help jumpstart your new habit of attitude each and every day:

1. **Each day, identify and be thankful for five of the seemingly smallest things that make a huge impact in your life.** This could be things like being able to hop on a plane and fly to a different state in just hours. Or having stocked grocery stores only minutes from home and a car that can get you there quickly. Smart phones allow you to communicate with family and friends immediately, at any time, anywhere in the world. Indoor plumbing, hugs from a son or daughter

before leaving for work, hot water, traffic lights that maintain sanity in our streets…are all small things to appreciate that we often overlook.

2. **Each day, appreciate one opportunity that you have to grow or make progress.** Opportunities are everywhere and present themselves daily. It is up to us to be open to seeing them. For example, email acts as a huge burden for many, until we learn new ways to better organize and manage the never-ending inbox. Learn to appreciate the freedom to read a book, learn a new skill, and be able to apply what you learned to your work or personal life. Learning how to be a better spouse, parent, friend, leader, contributor, or team player provides never-ending opportunities to make progress.

3. **Each day, appreciate one teacher in your life and learn a new lesson.** Most reading this probably are not in school, but the reality is we have teachers around us our whole life and are learning new lessons forever. Teachers might be the author of a book you read, a friend with a skillset or a quality you would like to have a speaker at a seminar you've attended, or a spouse who knows you better than anyone.

While there are hundreds of ways to practice gratitude, these three stand out to me. They require a bit more thinking and they have empowered me to pay much closer attention to the small things each day or week that I should be grateful for.

#10 - Create Your Not-To-Do List

Many of us start our day with a long list of "to-do" items. Even worse, we sabotage ourselves by creating a list far too long for any mere mortal to ever complete, leading to frustration and a never-ending feeling of not having enough time.

It is time to create your *Not-To-Do List*. This process of thinking through all of the things, or activities, or habits that you would like to get rid of or will no longer do can be much more freeing and productive than the typical list of goals and resolutions. The reality is, we all have enough time...we just don't prioritize it very well.

Action Steps:

1. **Start your Not-To-Do list.** Write down anything and everything you can think of that you would like to no longer do. Consider things that frustrate you at home or at work, or distract you from getting the results you desire. Keep this list close by so you can add to it whenever you think of more things. Here are some examples:

    - I will stop leaving my email inbox open all day
    - I will not check Facebook more than once per day
    - I will not work late so it forces me to skip my gym workout

- I will not lose valuable family time by doing yard work on the weekends
- I will not "veg out" in front of the TV every night of the week
- I will not spend time with people I do not enjoy being around
- I will not waste money on things that are not connected to my most important goals
- I will not have my children stare at the iPad or watch TV just because it is easier for me

2. **Choose your top twelve.** Now that you have a master list, choose the top twelve. It is extremely important to narrow your focus, even though you would love to stop doing everything on your list. Creating new habits, and eliminating old ones, can be very difficult and will take time. By choosing twelve, this will allow you to tackle one per month and twelve over the course of the year. This keeps your goals realistic and achievable while building momentum throughout the year.

3. **Convert each Not-To-Do item into an action plan.** The best way to eliminate a bad habit is to create a *new* habit that leaves no room for the one you are trying to escape. Looking at your top twelve, choose the first three that will be your goal over the next three months. Next, write an action plan that eliminates the

not-to-do item by creating a positive habit or activity. Here is an example of three not-to-do items from above converted to action plans for the first three months of the year:

- I will schedule three 30-minute blocks of time each day to check and respond to emails. I will notify all of my co-workers of these times and turn on an auto-responder in my Outlook.
- I will spend 30-60 minutes each weeknight before bedtime reading a book or playing games with my children.
- I will hire a yard maintenance company to come every other week so I can spend more quality time on the weekends with my family and friends.

To truly create a new habit, you must repeat it 21 times, hence your goal of just accomplishing one not-to-do item per month and three per quarter. It is better to only work on three items and accomplish them all than to tackle all of them at once and not accomplish any. Each quarter, choose three more items on your not-to-do list and follow step three above. By the end of your year, you will have eliminated twelve things in your life that caused you frustration and your life will be tremendously more enjoyable, productive and fulfilling!

#11 - Learning Proactive Gratitude

Every year, when the holidays come around, we are reminded everywhere we turn to "be grateful", and "give to others". But how do we go about living this way year-round? The key is to transition from "reactive" to "proactive" gratitude.

Reactive Gratitude

Most of us are programmed to give thanks and be grateful only when we receive something. This may be in the form of a gift from someone, a nice gesture someone does for us, or in the business world when we receive a great referral or introduction to a new client. If we are doing this right, then we quickly get a thank you card out or make a personal phone call to show "reactive" gratitude. Unfortunately, if you are like my kids when we force them to write thank you cards after a birthday, we can find ourselves causing our children to grow up thinking gratitude is a moral obligation rather than a way we should live our lives.

Proactive Gratitude

On the other hand, what if we created a habit of being proactively grateful, without the need for anything external to happen to us? Some of you may do this fairly well already, but many do not.

Proactive Gratitude can take many forms, but the simplest way to start is by listing 3-5 things you realize you take for granted every day. I'm grateful I can get into my car, turn the heater on, and drive myself to work each day. I'm grateful that I have a comfortable home to end each day in. I'm grateful that I can place my garbage right outside my house on the sidewalk each week for someone to pick it up. I am grateful when, after a long day at work, my wife has had the time to prepare an amazing meal that I can sit and eat with my family. I'm grateful I can flip a switch and have light, or turn on a faucet and have hot water!

These are not things I normally even think about as I rush around each day, complain when there's too much traffic, or curse the torrential and never-ending down pour of rain.

And guess what? It is impossible to be grateful and angry at the same time! Try it. Yes, you can switch back and forth if you try really hard, but in reality, as you are thinking through all that you are grateful for, you will find yourself less and less "angry" or frustrated by those other things.

Oh...and while I am on it, I am thankful for YOU! Thank you for reading, learning, and committing to a bigger future for you and those you love!

#12 - How Much Time Off Will You Take This Year?

Let me paint a picture...and decide if it defines you a bit too well, or someone you know well:

You wake up in the morning and out of habit, grab your smart phone next to your bed to check your emails. In the evening, you clean up dinner, put the kids to bed, and then settle in with your laptop to get another hour or two of work done. The weekend rolls around and your spouse and kids keep chastising you for checking your phone for work emails, or even worse...taking work calls.

So I ask the question: How much time OFF will you take this year?

Let's begin by defining a "day off". I define this as the time from when you wake up to the time you go to sleep. It means an entire day of no work activity, no checking work emails, and answering work-related calls, reading work-related materials, and even no writing down that genius idea you just had.

With this definition in mind, decide now how many days off you will take this year. Here's a hint: if you actually took the entire weekend off, that would add up to 104 days typically. Assuming you have two weeks of paid vacation you take, and you commit to making it a true vacation and not simply "working remotely", that might add another 10 days. This gets you to 114.

But figure out your number now, and write it down.

Why is this so important?

1. Rejuvenation
2. Productivity

First, rejuvenation. I want to retrain you on how to view time off from work. Taking time off is no longer a reward for killing yourself the prior five days, five weeks, or five months. Taking time off is a requirement to be at your best when you are at work AND when you are at home.

With this definition in mind, you owe it to your co-workers, your boss, and most importantly, your family. Taking a full weekend off, or a week of vacation somewhere, with absolutely no work, will rejuvenate you and help you show up to work rested and creative, ready to solve those difficult problems and be much more productive.

Speaking of productivity, let's move on to the second reason taking true, un-plugged time off is so important. Look at your number of days off you wrote down. For the sake of this lesson, let's assume you wrote down 114. This means you have 251 days left in the year to accomplish all of your work-related goals. Suddenly your mind realizes you don't have as much time as you thought and that you'd better get a move on. No more excuses for wasted days. No more time for not maximizing every day you're at work, getting the most out of each day and from each teammate or employee you supervise.

We all know that we are most productive the days leading up to a vacation. When time is scarce, it's amazing how productive we become. On the other hand, when we know we have all day or all week to get something done, we are automatically less focused and less determined, and more open to allowing interruptions and distractions into our day.

By first committing to taking "X" number of days off, you've now tricked your mind into realizing you have no choice but to get more done at work in less time. And it works. Now you're more productive at work, which then frees you up to actually take more time off!

#13 - How Are You Expanding Your Mindset?

This is a question I have challenged myself with each year, so I will ask you the same question:

How will you continue expanding your mindset?

First, why is this even important? I believe that how we think impacts virtually everything else in our lives. Our beliefs lead us to the actions we take and the choices we make. Where we are in life and everything we've achieved (or not achieved) so far is a direct result of the choices we've made. And my personal interactions with others on a daily basis confirm that most of us are not satisfied with our current results. There's always that "gap" from where we want to be and where we are today. So, simple math would say, we must expand our mindsets to continuously achieve growth, both personally and professionally.

And if that doesn't convince you, then consider that you'll be much more interesting to be around since you'll have many more interesting things to share and talk about!

If you need a head start on some ways to expand your mindset, here are the three primary ways I intentionally expand my mindset:

1. **Documentaries.** I set a fun and challenging goal of watching 52

documentaries in 2017. That basically meant averaging one per week. To do so would force me to take a break from my favorites like Homeland, Vikings, and Game of Thrones. With Netflix and Amazon Prime, it is very easy to expand your mindset by choosing a variety of documentaries on topics outside of your normal areas of interest. Set a goal of even one documentary per month! (By the way, I only reached half of my goal in 2017, but from the 26 I did watch, some have had a huge impact on my thinking around health, finances, and politics.)

2. **Reading.** This is an every-year goal of mine, as I am an avid reader. But I understand that very few people in this country read non-fiction books. All I can say is this: the most successful people in life tend to read a lot of books. If you're not a reader, it might be worth a try. Every year I set aside 12-15 non-fiction books I intend to read that year. Decide where you really want to improve your life and become a student! Try scheduling 15-30 minutes each morning to start your day. Even reading one non-fiction book per month puts you far ahead of probably most anyone you know.

3. **Journaling.** To be honest, this area has been a challenge for me to stick with. While I've dabbled in starting my day by journaling, I have not been able to stick

with it consistently. That was until I discovered *The 5-Minute Journal*. This journal provides a simple outline to start your day right and even encourages you to reflect at the end of each day on all the good that happened. It's a daily reminder that we can't be angry or depressed when we're being grateful for all that we have. In addition, I have started an additional journal where I only write down things that I have learned each day. So far it has been extremely helpful for me to write and capture one to three key takeaways from my morning ritual of reading, or highlights from an important conversation or podcast I listened to.

You can imagine there are countless ways to expand your thinking. Like anything in life, the key is committing to it. These are three ways I plan to intentionally expand my mindset throughout the year and beyond. My challenge to you is, how will YOU continuously expand your mindset and ensure that you grow and never stop learning? How will you create a habit of this daily or weekly?

We all owe it to ourselves, as well as to those around us, to never stop growing our mindset.

#14 - Stress and How to Overcome It

Here is my favorite definition of stress:

Stress is the gap between what we expect and what actually happens.

When we constantly compare our results (the "actual") with our expectations (the "ideal"), we will continue to find ourselves frustrated and over time, losing confidence.

- When we set a goal to lose twenty pounds, but only lose eight pounds, we experience frustration and stress.
- When we expect our spouse to send flowers to us at work for our anniversary, but they don't, we experience stress.
- When we expect an easy commute home from work but instead get stuck in traffic, we experience stress.
- When we set a big goal to pay off all of our consumer debt by the end of the year, but end the year with some still left, we experience stress.

Many of us are perfectionists. We set high expectations for ourselves and for those around us. Yet, this can become a recipe for a very stressful life, since we cannot control other's actions and ways of thinking.

So how do we counter this? Yes, we must set expectations in life. And yes, it is important to set goals (the bigger the better)! But once we place that stake in the ground to define where we want to go, or what we want to happen, we must learn to measure ourselves by our progress, not the ideal.

This means we celebrate the eight pounds we lost, the flowers waiting for us at home for our anniversary, the extra time in the car to unwind and listen to music, and all of the debt we DID, in fact, get paid off.

Rather than constantly comparing where you are today to where you wish you were, you must instead "turn around" and compare to where you were yesterday, last month, or even last year. Recognize your accomplishments so far, and the progress you've made toward your goals and expectations.

#15 - Life is Simply a Series of Events

Over the course of a day, we experience many "events". Throughout an entire year, we experience thousands and thousands of "events". An "event" could be a new client signing up, or it could be an accident on the freeway making us late for work, or your son or daughter missing the school bus that morning.

When we then choose to attach a label to each of these events, such as "good" or "bad" or "sad", we find ourselves on the emotional roller coaster that is known as life.

Yet, it is WE who choose to label these events as good or bad, positive or negative, sad or happy, etc.

Understanding that we control the labelling of these events suddenly gives me the emotional control to appreciate the unplanned opportunity to spend some additional time with my daughter as I drive her to school instead. I can choose to appreciate the extra time in the car, sitting in traffic, listening to an empowering book on CD or talking with a friend on the phone.

When you can take a pause, and sum things up as just another "event", you will find that the emotional roller coaster many of us are on throughout life suddenly settles down.

#16 - The Secret Word

Years ago, I read an incredible book that gave me an entirely new (and fun) way to coach my children to the best humans they can be. That's my job as a parent, right? The book is called"Aspire", and the author, Kevin Hall, explores the origins of impactful words and how they should apply to our lives.

The first chapter packs a punch by teaching what he calls The Secret Word, *'Genshai'* (pronounced GEN-shy).

This ancient Hindi word means that you should never treat another person in a manner that would make them feel small.

It's a big, important way to go through life, all packed into one cool word! I decided that I would begin teaching my children this "Secret Word" to live by at a young age. I will never forget the look of bewilderment on my then 6-year old daughter's face as I explained to her the meaning of *'Genshai'* on the way to school. She promptly asked, *"But, how can I make someone get smaller?"*

We both laughed as I realized the usage of the word "small" in this context didn't make sense to a child. So, I had to adjust the definition slightly to ***"Don't do or say things that will make other people feel bad about themselves."*** Years later, this word, or should I say, what to live, is a foundation for many lessons and learning opportunities as my children navigate school, sports, and various social circles.

Do you have a word that packs a punch like this one; "secret word" that re-focuses you, or your child, or your spouse? Feel free to borrow this one, since I'm sure it applies to many situations throughout your year. You might even want to pick up the book and make it a family read around the fireplace before bedtime.

#17 - How Can You Have More Fun at Work?

Interesting question, eh? It was one that was posed to me recently, and it really got me thinking. How about you?

In some ways, I make having fun a certainty at our company. Every 90 days we have a team outing to celebrate our progress over the past quarter. Teams are put together at the beginning of the year, along with a budget, and they get to come up with whatever they want for our entire team.

We also implemented the Awesomeness Jar. This is cheap and simple, but throughout the month every teammate is encouraged to recognize a co-worker who's gone above and beyond...or was "awesome". They then drop a nomination in the jar and at the end of the month, the most awesome person wins a fun little gift.

We also host Client Appreciation Events every other month, with fun themes like Rejuvenation, Mad Men, Old West, and 80's Rock. The office gets decorated, props are set out for guests, and we tend to have 30-50 business partners come each time to enjoy food, drinks, and a bit of networking. We even introduced an office corn hole set this year!

Those are just a few of the things that came to mind that we already do when I was asked this question. But what else could I do? What can YOU do to have MORE fun at work?

- Add some new decorations to your office or cubicle?
- List some new habits you want to create this year and track your progress?
- Let go of some of the activities that annoy you the most at work (assuming you're allowed to)?
- Take a more active role in something?
- Start a charitable event?
- Bring a golf putter and putting machine to work for break-time putt-offs?
- Corn hole, darts, foosball, pool table? With an ongoing tournament?
- Book club, to encourage learning and growth amongst your teammates?

Give it some thought. When you think about it, we tend to spend more time with our co-workers than anyone else. It can seem sad to put it that way...OR...we can make it fun and something far more than a J-O-B.

#18 - What if Life Started Tomorrow?

Imagine if everything up to this point in your life was simply "practice"? What experiences and lessons would you bring forward and build upon going forward? What burdens of the past would you be able to mentally let go of and forgive yourself (and others) for?

Imagine that those poor financial decisions you made when you were younger were merely stepping stones in helping you learn how to better manage your money once life really started. What if that business venture that failed wasn't actually a failure, but rather a warm-up in knowing what to do and not do when real life begins? The short sale or foreclosure you went through was simply education on how important it is to have more money saved in the bank. The conflicts with your spouse or children were just helping you master your marriage and parenting skills for when life really gets started.

How would your mindset shift if none of the past really mattered, and everything that was truly important for your life actually started tomorrow?

When you really think about it, we tend to carry a lot of baggage around with us. We allow our past to dictate many of our present and future decisions. The past keeps many of us from taking risks or pursuing big goals. We allow past failures to erode our confidence. And without confidence, we don't have the courage to do what we need to do to create a bigger, better future for ourselves.

View everything up to this point in your life as practice. Imagine your real life starts tomorrow and you get to choose the experiences and knowledge you want to bring with you. How will you approach it differently?

Money

#19 - Creating Your Best Money Year Ever

One of the primary reasons many people do not achieve financial success is they have never stopped to define what "financial success" means to them. Without a clear vision, how will you ever know if you actually ever *achieve* success?

The path to achieving the future you desire with your money can be viewed in three critical steps: **Vision, Goals**, and **Habits**.

Step 1: Create your Money Vision.

Start by answering this one question:

"Imagine it is one year from today. Looking back over the past year, what must have happened with your personal finances for you to be happy with your progress?"

As you answer this question, remember you are looking back from the future. Everything you say and write down has already happened! So, describe it in this way. For example, don't say, "I hope I have saved $5,000 in an emergency fund," or "I want to pay off my credit card." Rather say, "I *have* $5,000 saved in an emergency fund," and "I *have* paid off my Visa."

Step 2: List your top three to five Money Goals to accomplish this year.

With your vision in place, it is now time to narrow down your focus to the specific action items. Examples might include:

- Have $3,000 in savings for emergencies
- Get our college savings plan for my kids up to $5,000
- Pay off a car loan
- Save up $10,000 for a down payment on a new home
- Establish (and stick to) a monthly spending plan

Out of this list, try to choose the #1 goal that, if accomplished, will make the others easier or no longer necessary. Typically, one goal will be a catalyst to better accomplishing the others. For example, paying off a car loan may free up $400 per month to then "super-charge" your savings goals. Or, establishing a spending plan (a.k.a budget) might just be the necessary step to achieving any of the other goals.

Step 3: Establish the two "Money Habits", or actions, necessary for you to accomplish the #1 goal

This is where the rubber meets the road. What two habits, or actions, will you implement consistently to achieve this goal? These must be very specific, and ideally, you can put these habits into your calendar. Depending on your specific goal you have chosen to tackle first, here are some examples:

- Spend no more than $100 per week on groceries
- Put $250 per month into Emergency Fund
- Save 10% of my take-home pay each pay period into a separate savings account
- Contribute 5% of my gross income to my 401k at work
- Pay an additional $200 per month toward my car loan
- Review and discuss our family spending plan for 30 minutes each Sunday evening

The first step to achieving a bigger, better future for yourself and your family, is to go from "wishing" or "hoping", to planning and execution. Commit to your #1 goal and then have the courage to make the changes necessary to improve your financial life this year and every year!

#20 - Are You Playing the Right Money Game?

Too many people are playing the wrong game with money.

If we truly want to be successful with our personal finances, we must commit to learning how to make smarter financial decisions to better achieve our short and long-term goals. Becoming a student of proper cash flow and liability (a.k.a. debt) management can play a vital role in your financial success...or lack thereof if you don't. If someone was to ask me what the biggest mistake most people make throughout their lives as it relates to money, I would answer, *"They aren't playing the right game."*

Here are some examples of the *wrong* games that too many people are playing:

- The debt-free game
- The increasing income game
- The low-interest rate game
- The savings game

It's not that the above examples aren't important. They absolutely are. But they are components of the much bigger game we must play with money...Net Worth!

Net Worth = Assets - Liabilities

Assets are the thing things you own that are worth money. Put simply, let's say your assets (savings, checking, retirement, home value, autos, etc.) add up to $500,000. Assume your liabilities or money you owe to others (student loans, credit cards, mortgages, auto loans, etc.) add up to $400,000. Your net worth would be $100,000 ($500,000 - $400,000). Most people understand this concept and math pretty easily, even if they don't always understand how to play the game.

Why Net Worth as the Focus?

Generally speaking, a positive net worth gives you options. Making decisions that always work to increase your net worth over time will lead to more options and freedom with your money in the future. This could mean the financial freedom to change careers to something you enjoy, help your children get through college without being burdened with an avalanche of student loans, or a parent able to stay home with a new child.

So how do we make sure we are playing the proper game, and focusing on increasing our net worth overtime?

One of the first things to understand is how your weekly or monthly decisions with money impact your overall net worth (or possibly don't). Imagine you are preparing to buy a new home and you have $100,000 in your bank account from the sale of your previous home. Here's a question:

Does your net worth change depending on how much of that you decide to use for the down payment on the new house?

Think about it. You already have the $100,000 as an asset. If you shift all $100,000 over into your new home, you now have $100,000 of a different asset called "Home Equity". At the same time, you no longer have that $100,000 in your checking account. This is called a "net-worth neutral move". Often the new homebuyer is so focused on having less mortgage debt that they don't realize they are also reducing an asset they already had...their checking account.

What about moving $5,000 from your checking account to pay off the $5,000 you owe on your credit card. Does this impact your net worth? Nope, at least not at that very moment. Your assets went down by $5,000, but so did the amount you owe to others. It may have been a good decision, based on other factors such as interest rates, cash flow, etc. but now you realize that this single move does not impact your net worth – which is the real game to focus on.

The benefit, in this case, may come from now having no credit card payment, thus giving you greater ability to save more money each month...which absolutely increases your net worth!

#21 - Four Powerful Money Questions to Make THIS Year the Best

Every year it is a good idea to start thinking early about what you'd like to accomplish in the New Year to improve your money and personal finances.

Here are four "power" questions to consider if you really want to make THIS your best year ever.

1. **What do you want to accomplish THIS year with your money?**
    Share with your spouse, significant other or an accountability partner what specifically you'd each like to accomplish this year with your money. This will open up the money dialogue and get you both on the same page. Then, create a written list of the top three to five things, prioritizing by importance so you know which to tackle first. For best results, accomplish the #1 goal first before moving on to the next one.

2. **What frustrates you the most when it comes to your personal finances?**
    Discussing together what frustrates you the most should get you fired up to make some changes moving forward! Do you buy things on impulse? Do you overspend on dining out? Do the credit

card bills depress you? Stop settling for
mediocrity when it comes to your
financial future. Make a list of your
biggest money frustrations so you can
discuss and begin taking action to
eliminate them.

3. **What could you do to DOUBLE your savings THIS year over last year?**
As a nation, we are encouraged to spend
and consume. Trying to "keep up with the
Jones's" leads the majority of families to
live paycheck to paycheck. *It is time you
realized that you are in charge of your
personal economy!* Nobody else will
encourage you to save more, live debt
free, pay cash for vacations, and someday
enjoy the financial freedom few others
will have. So, it is up to you, and that
means saving more, and saving
consistently, every single month. It is up
to you to maintain the discipline needed
to make the necessary changes.

4. **What strategies have you already tried that have worked? What strategies have NOT worked?**
Personal finance is mostly about behavior
and choices. If you don't have much
money in the bank, look at the choices
you have made, and start making better
choices. Change your behavior and your
money situation will change too. *A goal
without implementation doesn't do
anybody any good!*

So, what happens if you DO NOT do this? You'll simply find yourself repeating the same goals, year after year, growing more and more frustrated at your lack of financial improvement. Do not waste another year wishing you had done more to improve your financial future. Discuss these four "power" questions so you can start creating your bigger, better future NOW!

#22 - How Do YOU Define Financial Safety?

This is a question I've studied and asked people for many years now. The answers vary and also tend to change over time.

So how do YOU define financial safety for yourself and for your family?

- Having no debt?
- Lots of money in savings?
- Enjoying a low-cost lifestyle?
- Being mortgage free?
- Earning a high income?
- Job security?
- Having lots of "stuff"?

What else? What, above all else, would help you sleep better at night and feel safe and secure when "life happens"? Because we all know it will.

Once you define what Financial Safety means to you, check to see if your choices with money are in alignment with this? For example, many people have shared with me that "money in the bank" is what makes them feel the safest, even over having no debt. Yet, when we look at where their left-over money is going each month, we often find extra payments being made toward the mortgage rather than going into savings. Just like that, a lightbulb goes off, and they re-focused their money. They have realized that even if things get really bad, such as a job loss or a financial emergency, money in the bank is far safer than pre-paying their mortgage. Not to mention, the only way to lose a house through foreclosure is by not having the cash to make the payments during tough times!

Decide what financial safety means to you and get to work building it and maximizing it. Put your money there first, then move on to other goals. There's not much worse than financial stress and anxieties around money.

Hint: Go deeper than your first answer. Often times the true definition for you personally is a few layers behind your initial thought.

#23 - 3 Steps to Creating the Financial Future You Want

Throughout life, I have found that when it comes to money, most people really want more freedom with their money, less financial stress, and more time to enjoy "life". If these financial goals are similar to yours, here are three mindset shifts you can make to achieve all three:

- Raise Your Standards
- Get Rid of Your Limiting Beliefs
- Change Your Strategy

Raise your Standards

If you really want to make changes that last, you must raise your standards. You must no longer accept living paycheck to paycheck as an option. You must no longer allow the question, "Where does all my money go?" come into your discussions. If you want to earn more money, and have more money in the bank, then expect to have it.

Change what you demand of yourself! On a sheet of paper, write down all the things you will no longer accept in your life when it comes to your finances. Will you continue to allow yourself and your family to live paycheck to paycheck? Will you accept not saving enough money each month for your child's college education or your own retirement? Then list everything you aspire to become, do, or have! Post it somewhere you will read daily.

Get Rid of Your Limiting Beliefs

Raising your standards without truly believing you can meet them will lead to failure. Your beliefs shape your actions as well as how you think and feel about everything. Your beliefs are determining what you think is possible or impossible in your life or with your money. Let's be honest...some people just don't believe they should have financial freedom or abundance. This may not be a conscious thought, but it's very likely it is a subconscious one.

One way to begin eliminating your limiting beliefs is by breaking your financial goals and dreams down into easy, manageable steps. If you want $10,000 saved for emergencies, start with $1,000 and build from there. Find a mentor. Read books. Track your progress to build confidence and gradually your limiting beliefs will erode.

Change Your Strategy

I will assume if you are reading this book, you are already committed to creating a bigger, better future for yourself and those you care about. The final step in doing this is making changes to your strategy. Applying some of the strategies found in this book, along with raising your standards and getting rid of limiting beliefs, by default you will be changing your strategy.

Remember, where you are today (financially, professionally, personally) is a result of the choices you have made up to this point. This means you have the control and the power to make different choices going forward. You are empowered. You can choose to spend a little less, ask for that raise, start a new business, and become better educated on personal finances.

Often, changing your strategy can be as simple as taking action! Most of us know what we should do, but few actually do it. Time is our most precious resource. Allocate more of your time in building a better, safer, more abundant financial future.

#24 - How to Gain Financial Clarity and Confidence with Money

For most, money is at the heart of your goals, since most goals involve either spending money, saving money, or paying down debt. So where should you start?

Here is a step-by-step money planning process that will give you clarity, confidence and direction this year, and every year.

1. **First, start with your money vision.**

   Grab a blank piece of paper or open up a blank document on your computer. Write at the top: ***"Imagine it is December (insert year)..."*** Now mentally project yourself into the future to the end of the current year. Perhaps it's January, or March, or even August. But now you're sitting by the fire, with the New Year celebration right around the corner, looking back over the previous months of the year. Write on your paper exactly what HAS to have happened for you to be happy with the financial progress. Just write, in free form, anything that comes to mind. This written document becomes your VISION for a successful year!

2. **Next, come back to present time and make a list of 7-10 goals you wrote down that involve money or finances.**

   These might include, *"Increase Savings"*, *"Pay Down Debt"* or *"Purchase a New Car"*. They don't have to be completely specific yet, just get them all written down, big and small. I call this the "brain dump".

3. **Armed with your list, now decide which your #1 is.**

   This can be difficult since all probably seem important. What this means is, out of all of your money goals, there should be one that stands out; one that trumps all others, and if accomplished, would make all the others easier or no longer necessary. For example, "Increase Savings" would allow you to "Purchase a New Car" faster and easier, or start a child's college savings account, or save up for a vacation you want to take.

4. **With your #1 goal now identified, choose how you will measure your success or failure.**

   If your goals aren't specific and measurable, you will most likely fail. That's just how goal setting and achievement works. Give a number to your goal that will be how you measure your progress...and ultimately your success. For example, if your #1 money goal is paying off debt, your first number to measure your success by might be: "Zero balance on the Alaska Visa". There's no longer any ambiguity to your goal. When December 31st arrives, you either have a zero balance or you don't, right? With this kind of goal, you may even have a second number, such as: "Only $5,000 left on auto loan". Having at least two ways to measure your progress around your top goal is key to your ability to achieve it.

6. **Finally, write down two key activities or behaviors that you will implement to achieve the above results.**

   This is where the rubber meets the road. This is where you must commit to a behavior that will determine whether you achieve your goal or not. New habits might be, "Pay $500 extra on the Alaska Visa each month," or "Limiting weekly grocery budget to $200." Both of these are action items you can control and push you towards your goal.

You've now taken an important goal in your life and built a plan to achieve it. The best part is, you can now also measure whether you're on track throughout the year rather than waiting until it is too late and realizing you failed. Now apply this process to your other goals as well!

#25 - Look Far, Look Near, and Look in Your Rearview Mirror

If you took driver's education in high school, you may remember this mantra! The idea is to focus on these three key areas as you drive. "Look far" means look way up ahead at what's happening with traffic. "Look near" means pay attention to the cars and pedestrians immediately in front of you and beside you. "Look in your rearview mirror" obviously means to constantly check what is happening behind you.

Years later I now realize this fun and catchy saying can also be a valuable technique in planning your personal finances.

- **Look far:** This suggests the absolute importance of setting long-term goals and defining your Ideal Lifestyle. By creating a compelling vision of how you want your life to be, and where you are trying to get to, you can better focus your money activities today. With a clearly defined vision, you can more easily prioritize your spending, align your savings GOALS with what's most important to you, and stay motivated to pay off your debt as fast as possible.
- **Look near:** From a financial point of view, this describes important activities such as tracking your spending habits, investing for retirement and setting up a

college savings plan for your children. It is about assessing your daily, weekly, and monthly cash-flow and making sure your spending habits and savings goals are aligned with your Ideal Lifestyle!

- **Look in your rearview mirror:** I have often coached on the importance of "Review, Reflect, and Reward". It teaches you the importance of looking back on your achievements and acknowledging what you have accomplished. It is also about reflecting on your greatest struggles and how you did, or will, overcome them. And finally, you must reward yourself for your successes. Creating rewards for yourself and your growth or progress around your most important goals keeps you motivated when times get tough.

Make this a quarterly exercise for yourself and your family. Schedule some time every 90 days, maybe a Sunday evening, to review your long-term goals, short-term goals, and reflect on what you've accomplished and made progress on so far. It will build confidence and keep you on track!

#26 - How Much Should You Keep in Your Cash Reserves?

Depending on what book you read, or financial guru you listen to, the answer to this question will vary quite a bit. So, the quick answer is, it depends on you.

Many financial professionals suggest that you put away somewhere between three to six months' worth of your normal living expenses for emergencies. We actually call these funds "Cash Reserves", because the reality is, most things that might happen are not really emergencies. Once established, I also refer to this as your "sleep well at night" account!

If you lose your job, or become disabled and don't have adequate disability insurance, you'll need that money to pay your regular monthly expenses, such as mortgage payments, insurance premiums, groceries, and car payments, until you can find another job. Without such an emergency fund or Cash Reserves, a period of unemployment could put your assets at risk. If you miss too many mortgage payments, your house and the equity in your house could be taken through foreclosure. Similarly, if your car breaks down or your spouse has a medical emergency, you'll want to have the necessary cash to pay the bills. You don't want to be faced with an immediate need for cash, only to discover that you don't have any.

So, the answer to how much you should set aside depends really on some key criteria:

- How secure is your job? The less confident you are, the more cash you should sock away.
- Does your spouse work and earn money, or do both of you? If you have two income sources, your risk is lower if one person loses their job.
- How do you get paid? If a portion of your income fluctuates, such as commissions, or bonuses, or tips, you definitely want to be prepared for those "winter months" or slow times. They always come, so shoot for more money in your Emergency Fund.

If you are struggling to get Cash Reserves established, start with a small goal. Work toward $1,000, then gradually build toward $5,000. For more help on this, read the lesson "How to Prioritize Your Cash Flow".

Where should you store your Cash Reserves? Really any type of account that maximizes Safety (it will be there when you need it) and Liquidity (easy to access quickly). Rate of return is less important. You may have already set up an emergency fund. Did you put the cash in a five-year certificate of deposit (CD) or other long-term investment? In an emergency, you will need to get at those funds immediately. You can certainly pull your money out of the CD early, but you'll pay a penalty. It's better to keep some funds more liquid, in a traditional savings account, a money market deposit account, or a six-month CD, for example. That way, the cash will be readily available when you need it.

Finally, keep your cash reserves separate from your everyday accounts. This money is NOT a glorified checking account, where you are constantly moving money back and forth. You might even want to use a different bank. Unless you are extremely disciplined, you'll be tempted to spend those extra funds if you keep them in your checking account. Remember, if you can put off an expense until next week, it is probably not an emergency.

Set your goal for Cash Reserves, then map out a plan to get there. No goal is unrealistic, just be patient and set realistic timeframes.

#27 - How to Prioritize Your Cash Flow

We live lives of cash flow! This is a mantra you can repeat daily to yourself and those around you. Whether you are preparing to buy (and finance) a new house soon, or already own a home and are trying to build your savings and pay off debt, here is a simple yet powerful formula to follow as money flows in and out of your bank account.

1. **First Priority: Establish Your Cash Reserves:**

    Sometimes referred to as emergency funds, this is a sum of money that acts as the foundation for your financial safety. The best place to usually store Cash Reserves is in a savings account. Interest rate is not the most important factor for this money. Rather, safety and liquidity are...meaning, will the money be there when I need it, and can I get to it fast in the case of an emergency. Set a target or goal for how much you would like to have saved in your Cash Reserve account and start putting your first dollars of savings toward this. For some, this may be three months of your living expenses or six months of your income. Whatever it is, agree with your spouse on an amount that you both will feel good if achieved. For example, if your goal is $10,000, then any extra cash goes into this fund until you reach $10,000. If you allocate $200, or $500 per month in your budget to save, then that first goes to fund your Cash Reserves.

2. **Second Priority – Pay Off Consumer Debt:**

   Once your Cash Reserve goal is met, start attacking that consumer debt! The temptation will be to pay down the debt first since the interest rates are higher. The problem with putting too much money toward debt eliminating consumer debt before you have sufficient savings is that "life" will happen. Just as you get close to paying off that high-interest credit card, your transmission will go out. Without the savings, you'll be forced to charge back up your credit card that you just worked so hard to pay down. Thus, if you have $500 available each month, and your Cash Reserves are in place, then begin paying extra toward either the smallest debt or the debt with the highest interest rate. It is typically best to NOT spread the $500 across multiple debts.

3. **Third Priority: Build Your Liquidity (Savings and Investing):**

   With your Cash Reserves in place and your consumer debt out of the way, it is time to super-charge your savings. Hopefully along the way you've already been contributing to an employer retirement account, but if not, start there. Talk to your trusted financial advisor if you do not have one. Building your Liquidity can mean saving for your children's college, increasing your retirement contributions, and even saving for the next year's vacation so you can pay cash and not charge it. Remember, the real money game of life is 'net worth'. All of your decisions should be focused on increasing your personal financial safety, and then growing your net worth. Think how nice it would feel to have a year's worth of your living expenses saved up!

4. **Priority Four: Pay Off Your Mortgage**

This is a tricky one. Helping families finance their homes for nearly two decades now, I have seen a lot of mistakes on this level. Rather than go into depth on this lesson, in order to keep it from getting too long, I'll leave you with this strategy: pay off your mortgage *only* after the first three priorities are taken care of, and you find yourself in the home that you look forward to retiring in and being mortgage free in.

This simple but very effective model will improve your confidence with money and build the safest path to financial freedom and peace of mind.

#28 - Spend Less, So You Can Save More

Reducing your spending is the fastest way to increase your ability to save for your future. But to really make a difference, and know where you can cut back, you first need to know where your money goes. A great (albeit somewhat painful) strategy is to keep track of all your expenses for a month.

Set a goal for 30 days, and track everything. No expenses are too small or insignificant: the daily newspaper, coffee on the way to work, an extra gallon of milk, that burger at the fast-food outlet. Next, categorize the expenses so you can see what you spend and where you spend it. Be sure to factor into your monthly expenses a prorated portion of the annual cost of your irregular expenses (e.g., clothes, gifts, car maintenance, and insurance premiums).

Keep in mind that it is rarely the big-ticket items that get in our way of saving more and building our net worth. Most often it's the small expenditures, made over and over throughout the month that seems menial, that add up over time. These small expenses are also the best place to start in cutting back our spending, so we can save more.

Expenses generally fall into two categories. Essential expenses are ones you can't avoid (e.g., mortgage or rent, utilities, groceries, car insurance). Discretionary expenses are ones you choose to incur (e.g., eating out, entertainment, gifts, cable, travel). Discretionary expenses are the ones over which you will have the most control.

- Do you buy a lot of books? Try the library instead.
- Take coffee or lunch to work rather than buy it once you get there.
- Limit eating out to once a week rather than twice.
- Instead of going to the movies, rent one.
- Cancel subscriptions you rarely use.
- Although essential expenses are fixed, there may be ways to reduce them. Make sure you shut off the lights and TV when you leave the room.
- Change the oil in your car on a regular basis to avoid more costly repairs due to neglect.
- Review your insurance policies: Can you save on your premiums?
- Only grocery shop with a list. It's been proven you spend less when focused on only what you need.

Many of these may be very small adjustments. That's ok. That also means they are easy to make. And the little changes add up to big results over time.

Pick a realistic goal for your monthly spending reduction and try not to make too many changes all at once. To see how big a difference this can make, do the math. If you start by committing to reduce your spending by $2 a day, that's $730 a year! Set the saved money aside, perhaps in a savings account for your planned vacation, or use it for a specific purpose, such as reducing debt faster.

#29 - The Easiest Way to Save More Money

Sometimes we make money more complicated than it needs to be. If your goal is to save more money, but you constantly find yourself making excuses why you can't, it is time to simplify things.

What is the easiest way to save more money? Never let it touch your hands!

This sounds simple, right? It is if you take a few necessary steps to automate your savings and leave your personal decision-making out of it. Sometimes the economic conditions drive us to either save more or spend more. When we feel confident about things, we tend to spend more. When we are nervous, or even downright scared about where things are heading (think of the housing meltdown of 2007 – 2009), or about our job situation, we tend to save more to compensate for the uncertainty that lies ahead. During scare times, we tend to watch our spending more carefully, and recommit to building up more cash reserves.

But how do we make sure we are saving plenty of money regardless of market and economic trends?

Save your money before it even comes to you.

Set up your savings to automatically come out of your paycheck before you get it. The reason work-place retirement programs, such as 401(k) or 403(b), work so well is that the money you invest comes out of your paycheck before going into your bank account or into your hands. You can do the same for your personal savings goals. Determine how much you want to save each month, and do one of the following:

1. Have your employer direct-deposit a portion of your income each month into a separate savings account. Many employers have this ability...just ask.
2. Have your bank or credit union auto-transfer money from your checking account to a separate savings account after each paycheck goes in. This can be easier than option #1 and works great if your employer cannot split up your paycheck.

If you still manually receive paychecks that you must physically go to the bank and deposit...get out of this habit as soon as possible. Set up direct-deposit with your employer and automate your savings.

Save your raises and bonuses.

Here's another tip for once you set your savings on "auto-pilot": The next time you get a monthly pay raise, increase your monthly savings by that same amount! Stop the bad habit of just increasing your lifestyle and instead, put those extra dollars towards your financial future and safety. Learn to live below your means, so that when you do make more money, you enjoy the luxury of instantly being able to increase your personal savings rate.

There are many experts that argue better savers are happier people. While there is no guarantee you will be happier, I'm sure you would agree that NOT saving enough can easily detract from happiness. A lack of savings, and overall feeling of financial security can be difficult on marriages and relationships.

Save more now by removing the temptations of having the money in your hands. Combine this strategy with tracking your net worth each month, and your confidence will grow as you watch your net worth grow! Plus, if an unexpected money need pops up, you will be more prepared than ever before and no longer be forced to take out that credit card you just paid off.

#30- -The Three Choices You Have With Every Dollar

With every dollar you have, there are only three things you can do with it:

1. **Spend it**
2. **Save it**
3. **Pay down debt with it**

This applies to really any amount of money you might have or will have. What do YOU do with your money? How do YOU make the important decision every day on whether you will spend your money, save it, or pay down debt with it? What knowledge do you rely on to help ensure you are making the best decision each time so that you are on the right path to your financial goals?

As most statistics show, the average savings rate in America is dismal. I usually see 2% of people's income as the average. This then means that 98% of people's income goes to spending or paying down debt. Given the fact that Americans typically have far more debt than they should, it goes to reason that the majority of money is allocated to spending.

There is nearly unlimited advice on what you should do with your money each month. In general, you probably already know that you (and all of us) should be spending less and saving more. Sounds simple, right? Yeah, simple, but not always easy...

Take a little time to determine how much of your money goes toward each of the three options. It helps to block out one hour and log in to your bank accounts online or look at your monthly statements over the last three months.

Look at how much you deposited, or brought in. Then, review how much of your money went OUT in the form of spending, or paying down debt, or hopefully even into a separate savings account! Also, count any money that went into your employer's retirement fund that you contributed pre-tax from your paycheck...that counts for saving!

Once you have the totals for spending, saving, and paying down debt, convert them into a percentage. For example, let's say you bring home (deposited, after-tax income) $5,000 per month. Then you determine that $2,200 goes to debt payments (mortgage, auto loan, credit cards); and you have $500 automatically transfer into a savings account each month as well. The rest gets spent on discretionary and non-discretionary items (food, gas, insurance, gifts, utilities, etc.). Here would be your results as a percentage:

- 44% of your money goes to pay down debt ($2,200 dived by $5,000)
- 10% of your money goes to saving ($500 dived by $5,000)
- 46% of your money is spent ($2,300 divided by $5,000)

How do the numbers feel when you see them? How can you increase your savings and spend less? Are there ways to better manage your debt to eventually be debt free of everything but the mortgage?

There is no right answer here as to what your percentages should be, but awareness goes a long way to improving habits around what we do with our money each and every month! Remember, what gets measured typically improves.

#31 - The 3 Reasons Budgets Fail

Nobody likes budgeting. It ranks right up there with root canals, dieting and cleaning out gutters. If we all had it our way, we'd have so much positive cash flow each month we wouldn't need to have a budget. Even then, we've all seen famous athletes and celebrities filing for bankruptcy after earning millions throughout their career.

According to most financial experts, the three primary reasons budgets fail are:

1. Lack of commitment and self-discipline
2. Setting unrealistic goals
3. A serious emergency (losing a job, divorce, illness) that destroys any set budget

I'm sure you can relate to these all too well. Reasons number one and two can be fixed. The third reason can at least be minimized with substantial savings to protect your budget

Why is a Budget Important?

Having a budget in place allows you to confidently and consistently pay for what you need and save up for what you want. This is the simplest way to think of the fundamental reason we must have a budget in place. Even if you find it difficult to always stick to it month after month, it is far better than having no budget, and no idea where your hard-earned money goes each month.

Setting Financial Goals

What goals do you have? What financial goals do you want to focus on? For most families, there are three main "buckets" to think about: spending, saving, and giving. Spending is easy, as we all do more than our fair share of this one. But from a goal standpoint, the spending "bucket" refers to short-term, smaller goals to have money available for, such as social activities with friends, birthday gifts, school clothes for the kids, and even upcoming weekend trips. "Saving" would be for more expensive, mid- and long-term items such as a summer camp your child wants to attend, a new car, and family trips. This also would include saving for your children's college, investing, and saving for a down payment on a new house.

For now, set a time to discuss what a budget is and why it is important. If your kids are old enough, include them. If you already have one, even if you need to blow off the dust that has accumulated on it, take time to review it and make adjustments where needed. Let your children see how you use a budget to run the household, pay bills, save for vacations, and pay for all of the great things they get to enjoy.

Then, discuss your financial goals. Create a list of things you want to save for and how this fits into your budget. This is crucial in overcoming the number one reason listed above on why budgets fail. By getting emotionally committed to a financial goal, you will be much more disciplined.

If you find yourself setting really big, seemingly unrealistic financial goals (see reason #2 budgets fail), you can overcome this by setting realistic time frames. You will not cure your bad spending habits overnight. But you can over time.

To minimize the risk of reason #3 above for why budgets fail, be sure your budget includes a proactive plan to save and build your Cash Reserves. Having money on hand, easily accessible, allows you to better deal with unexpected emergencies without completely derailing your budget.

More than anything, a budget should be the best tool you have to ensure you are NOT spending everything you earn and keeping a focus on your savings so you can build your net worth.

#32- -First Step – Stop Digging

Famous investment guru and billionaire Warren Buffett once said that if you find yourself in a hole, the first thing you must do is "stop digging".

While this sounds basic, people every day are digging themselves deeper and deeper into debt. They are spending more money each month than they bring home from their paychecks.

If you are serious about changing your financial future and getting on the right track to enjoy more freedom with your money, then you must stop negative spending habits! You must commit to ending this bad habit now. Debt and overspending have an incredibly negative impact on your financial future as well as your relationships and marriage.

If you have consumer debt now, what is your PLAN to pay it off? Do you have a PLAN? Do you know WHEN your debt will be completely paid off at your current rate of repayment?

How about your cash flow? Do you know to the dollar how much money you bring home each month? Do you know exactly how much is going out?

Which scenario sounds better?

1. You and your spouse are always bickering over money and you constantly feel the stress of living paycheck to paycheck.

2. You live within your means; have money in savings, and you and your spouse's money arguments have ceased.

Here are some critical first steps to help you STOP DIGGING and START PLANNING.

- Set goals. Set aside one evening with your spouse and write down your short, mid-, and long-term goals. These can be directly about money or not...but just about every goal seems to involve money in one way or another.
- Identify your total take-home pay. You should know this automatically, but if you do not, locate your last couple of pay stubs and see how much comes home each month, after taxes and retirement contributions at work.
- Identify how much you spend each month. To be as accurate as possible, you should track your expenses every month. Many expenses vary month-to-month.
- Identify your POSITIVE or NEGATIVE monthly cash flow. Do you spend more than you make? If not, how much is left over?

Commit to yourself, your family, and your future, to follow these steps over the next TWO WEEKS and develop a PLAN to STOP DIGGING!

#33 - Debt--the Good, the Bad, and the Ugly

There are three types of debt: "Good", "Bad", and "Ugly". Let's discuss the differences and provide some direction for addressing your debt-related issues.

But before we dive in, let's agree to one thing: No shame, no blame. Too often people express a sense of guilt or shame when they owe money. While I absolutely want you to be free of all "bad" and "ugly" debt, let's be clear on one thing: some types of debt are defensible, perhaps even desirable. So, let's dispense with the guilty complex and the destructive habits of blaming past bad decisions and focus on greater clarity and understanding of debt.

Good Debt

For the purpose of this lesson, I will define "good" debt as any debt that leverages an asset that increases in value over time. That really narrows it down, eh? For most families, this comes down to just one type of debt – a mortgage used to secure their house. Historically, house values increase over time and have helped many people achieve wealth and financial safety. To get that house, a mortgage was needed. Other good debts could include a business loan to help an owner grow their business or a commercial loan to secure a commercial building that generates income and increases in value over time. But for most reading this book, it comes down to just one type of debt...a residential mortgage.

Note: I'll also include student loan debt for a student IN school currently. Once they're out, see the next section.

Other possible kinds of good debt include loans for education since the debt increases future earning; automobile debt, if you cannot possibly buy a car for cash and don't buy more car than you need, even at 0% interest; and, in rarer circumstances, debt incurred for investment purposes.

Bad Debt

Bad debt generally includes car loans (the longer the term, the worse the debt), boat loans, vacation house loans (interest is possibly deductible, but you are also probably not using the house enough to be carrying debt on it)-- anything involving the payment of interest that is unreasonably high, that is not tax-deductible, or that is not for "essentials."

And here I will also include student loan debt for anyone who has since graduated and now is out in the working world. This debt is now in the "bad" debt category.

Ugly Debt

Put as simply as possible: Unpaid credit card balances constitute the absolute worst kind of debt imaginable. Just as compounding interest works meaningfully to your advantage when you are saving for retirement, the compounding of credit card interest charges puts you on a debt treadmill that can be very difficult to escape. While difficult, it certainly is not impossible. I've included lessons on paying off your "ugly" debt in this book in fact.

Of course, any judgment or collection on anything is "ugly" too, and most likely crushing your credit score. So, clean that up as soon as possible.

As you look at your debt, and take inventory to decide what to pay down or off first, use this guide. Attack the "ugly" debt first, and then move on to the "bad" debt. And then, contrary to some beliefs, hit the pause button before paying extra on that "good debt".

#34 - Debt Happens – It's How You Repay It That Matters

Whether it's your mortgage, money owed for home improvements, car loans, student loans, or last months' vacation still on your credit card, most of us have debt.

Debt comes and goes. You pay off everything, and then decide to remodel your kitchen. Your paid-off car finally breaks down and you need to get a new one.

Debt is a part of our lives. But having debt is not necessarily the problem. ***How you pay back your debt is what counts.***

With that being said, do you have a DEBT REPAYMENT plan? Everyone wants to be debt free...but rarely do they have a specific, measurable, and actionable plan to achieve this goal. And without a plan, goals can rarely be achieved.

How to get started

There are many ways to tackle your debt. So, I will just share my favorite and the one that has worked for me and many of my clients throughout the years:

1. List all of your debts. Include your balance, interest rate, and minimum payment due each month.
2. Put in order from either highest balance to lowest balance OR highest interest rate

to lowest interest rate. (HINT: If you're not sure which is better and have no preference, I recommend sorting by balance.)

3. Determine how much extra cash flow each month you can commit to paying off your debt. Whether it's $50 per month or $500 per month, just decide.

4. Starting with the debt that you owe the smallest balance on, pay the minimum plus whatever more you committed to each month until it is completely paid off. Along the way, pay only the minimum payment to the rest on your list!

5. Once it is paid to $0, assign the entire payment you have been applying to this now paid off debt, and apply it to the next debt up on your list with the next smallest balance owed! For example, if you had been paying $300 toward the smallest debt and only the minimum $50 each month to the next largest debt owed, you will now pay $350 per month to the next debt in line!

Continue this process of "rolling up" the entire payment to the next debt on your list until everything is paid off! This is commonly called the Debt Snowball. The best thing is, it dramatically speeds up your ability to be debt free without impacting your other money beyond the extra you committed to pay each month.

Give it a go! As I said in the beginning, debt will come and go. Things happen. When they do, just reassess who you owe money to, list them in order, and apply this process. Now you won't just be wishing you could get out of debt...you'll be working with a proven, consistent plan.

#35 - What Do You Have to Show For It?

If you ever needed a good kick-in-the-pants to really start making the changes necessary to improve how you handle your money and make sure you are laying the groundwork for a secure financial future, this is for you.

Step One: To start, have you ever looked up how much money you have actually earned over your entire life? If not, it is time. You can do this through the Social Security Administration's website (www.ssa.gov at the time of this writing). It takes only a few minutes to create a secure account and quickly you will be staring at your lifetime earnings total. It may be a shocker. The total includes all money you've reported as earnings clear back to your first job as a teenager. Enjoy the piece of confidence for a moment before moving on to step two.

Step Two: Now we must determine what we have to show for all this money we have worked so hard to earn over our lifetime. I want you to calculate your Net Worth. If you already have done this, pull it out now and update it. This will really identify what you have to show for all the money you have earned throughout your entire working life.

If you have never calculated your Net Worth, see the lesson: ***Are You Playing the Right Money***

Game". This lesson walks you through how to calculate your net worth.

How does your net worth compare to your lifetime earnings? Is it a number you are proud of or discouraged by? Is it better or worse than you thought it would be? If you are like me, it was downright deflating. To see how much money has been earned over the years, and for most of us, how little we have to show for it in relation is a definite downer.

What I hope this does is motivate you! This exercise is to bring absolute clarity on where you are today, and what's possible. Once the initial shock wears off at the disparity between what you have earned and what you now have to show for it in the form of your net worth, it is time to get to work on creating better money habits and building a more secure and abundant financial future.

Regardless, this is just a starting point. This actually should empower you. When you see just how much you have actually earned throughout your working life, you can better understand that whatever your money problems might be, it hasn't been due to earnings. It typically is a result of what happens to the money once it's in your hands. But now it is time to let go of the past. No shame, no blame. Pretend that everything leading up to today was practice, and the real money game starts TODAY!

- Where will you commit to spending a little less?
- How much will you commit to saving EVERY single month, whether it's $10 or $1,000 BEFORE you spend anything or pay your bills?
- What are your savings goals? Get emotionally committed to making a change.

Focus on net worth. It is simple, but definitely not easy. The first step is committing to a bigger, better financial future. The second step is having the courage to make necessary changes.

Mortgage

#36 - The Two Biggest Mistakes Home Buyers Make (and How to Avoid Them)

In the complex world of residential mortgages, many mistakes are made by home buyers as they try to navigate all of their options. The good news is, many of the mistakes are avoidable with some education and greater awareness. Here are the two biggest mistakes we see home buyers make when obtaining a mortgage, and a brief solution on how you can avoid them:

1. **The Commodity Trap:** Over the years, people have been led to believe that getting a mortgage is similar to buying milk at the store or ordering fast food through a drive-through window. Online lenders promote fast, digital processes that allow you to borrow hundreds of thousands of dollars all over your computer or phone.

    The reality is, the mortgage is likely the largest amount of money people will ever attempt to borrow. Once obtained, a mortgage becomes the biggest debt burden most people will ever carry. As a result, the monthly payment on that mortgage now typically becomes the largest expense on your family's budget each month. On the plus side, the mortgage helps us obtain perhaps the largest single asset (the house) that most people will ever enjoy and benefit from.

- **So, what is the solution?** Take the process of obtaining a mortgage seriously. Start early. Be educated by a mortgage expert who asks the right questions and takes the time to help you develop a plan for the best mortgage strategy. Do not rush the process or wait to begin the process once you've found a house you hope to buy. With the clock ticking on a closing date, you will ultimately leave yourself no time for proper planning and decision making that may have far-reaching consequences for the rest of your financial future.

2. **Compartmentalizing:** The second mistake refers to people not seeing the "forest through the trees". Uneducated buyers, whether it's their first house or fifth house, fail to see how critical the role is that mortgage can play in whether or not you achieve your ideal financial future. Instead, most people are taught to approach the process of obtaining a mortgage from the standpoint of, "Get me the cheapest mortgage and hurry up...I'll then figure out the rest of my finances and goals." They have not yet realized that how you structure a mortgage, and then how you decide to repay it over the

course of your lifetime, will dramatically impact every other aspect of your financial future.

- **So, what is the solution?** Stop segmenting your mortgage from other debts and goals you have. Understand that your mortgage, student loans, auto loans, credit cards, etc. are all debt. Some is "good debt", meaning you may get some tax benefits or it is being used to leverage an asset (house), and some is "bad debt". The ultimate goal is to minimize our overall cost of borrowing on ALL of your debt and maximize your cash flow.

Your house, and the accompanying mortgage must be factored into your overall short and long-term financial goals. If done wrong, it can seriously impede your ability to achieve your other goals. If done right, it can be a primary factor, a tool in a way, in helping you achieve the financial future you desire.

#37 - How to Manage Risk as a Homeowner

If you've ever met with a trusted Financial Advisor, one of their favorite questions is, "What is your risk tolerance?" This is also an important question when getting a mortgage and repaying a mortgage for years to come.

The first step in deciding on the right mortgage strategy for you is to first determine what type of loan you need to meet your goals. What this step really involves is answering the question, ***"How do I manage risk?"***

A fixed-rate mortgage comes with less risk than an adjustable rate mortgage. That seems obvious to most. But what about a loan product that is fixed for the first five years, and then converts to an adjustable rate mortgage (ARM) in year six? What about a 15-year fixed rate mortgage compared to a 30-year fixed rate mortgage?

It may come as a surprise that a 30-year fixed rate mortgage comes with a price. While you've ensured the lowest risk possible, having a bank guarantee you an interest rate and payment that never changes for 30 years, means you are paying a premium on the rate up front.

On the other hand, choosing a mortgage with a fixed interest rate for the first five, or seven, or even ten years, and then has the ability to adjust with the market, comes with a discount for you during those initial fixed-rate years. In return, you would be accepting possible risk in the future when the interest rate can fluctuate up or down depending on market conditions.

There is the emotional aspect to consider as well. When it comes to risk, some people just can't sleep at night knowing their interest rate, and monthly mortgage payment might change years down the road. This is fine. It's great to know your risk tolerance!

So why would anyone take on the additional potential risk for a lower initial interest rate? What if your last child is about to graduate from high school in two more years, and you and your spouse have every intention to sell your house and downsize to a nice condo on the river? Might it make sense to enjoy a discounted rate that may only last three or five years, knowing your plans involve selling and moving before the interest rate ever adjusts? What if your income will be increasing in the coming years, but right now you would benefit from a lower monthly mortgage payment?

Choosing the right mortgage product to best manage your risk tolerance is very important. Many homeowners do not realize there are a variety of mortgage products that may fit your needs and goals. With just about any investment there is risk. It's impossible to eliminate it all together. The best that you can do is to understand the products available to you and determine which one will provide you the confidence and peace of mind you desire.

#38 - How Much Can, and Should, You Borrow?

I always explain to new clients that there are two conversations to have:

1. What CAN you do?
2. Then, what SHOULD you do?

Primarily this applies to those about to begin the home buying process, and the first question you might ask is, "How much can I qualify for?" This question of how much mortgage you qualify for will be based on many factors, such as:

- How much money do you make?
- How do you get paid?
- How much down payment do you have?
- How long have you been at your job?
- How's your credit?
- What other debts and financial obligations do you have?

Armed with this information, and everything else that goes into completing a mortgage loan application, a lender can let you know how much you CAN borrow.

While this is an important step in determining what you qualify for to begin shopping for a house, it is nowhere near as important as how much you SHOULD borrow.

The most important factor in deciding how much you borrow on a mortgage is the accompanying monthly mortgage payment. For most of us, your mortgage payment is the single largest line item on your budget each month. Borrowing too much, just because a bank says you qualify to do so, to the point you no longer have the extra cash flow to save and invest each month, is a poor financial decision. Yes, the house over time should be an incredible investment. But it cannot be your only investment if you want to have a well-rounded portfolio.

Just remember that mortgage lenders do not factor in how much you spend on kid's activities, dining out, going on vacations, or even how much you invest into your employer's retirement plan for your future. What you qualify for is based on limited information, so it is up to you to make sure how much you borrow on a mortgage does not impede your other short and long-term financial goals!

This is where a true mortgage planning professional can play an instrumental role in your life. Learning what you CAN do is a fairly simple and quick process. But going through the strategic planning and thinking steps to determine what you SHOULD borrow, given your other financial goals and concerns, is much easier with a trusted professional with the right tools. Don't try to figure it all out alone.

#39 - The House versus Home Conversation

All too often people use emotion when making important financial decisions regarding how to finance their new home or repay their mortgage over time. Thus, a fun discussion to have with new home buyers and homeowners is what we call *"House versus Home"*.

It goes like this: *"When you hear the word 'home', what words come to mind?*

(Take a moment and think about what your answers are to this question.)

Often people will list things like 'family', 'neighbors', 'holidays', 'freedom', 'security', and so on. They begin to realize that the word 'home' tends to represent the emotional aspects of owning real estate. Put another way, they are the experiences you will have in a house.

Next, ask yourself: **"When you hear the word 'house', what words come to mind?**

Words like 'appreciation', 'mortgage', 'leverage', 'fixing the roof' and 'tax benefits' begin to describe the logical aspect of owning a house. The word "house" makes us think more of a physical shelter.

A home provides a place to raise a family, enjoy hobbies, socialize, sleep, relax, and more. Your sense of home comes from the experience you have living in your house, not necessarily from the house itself.

A house is a physical shelter made of concrete, wood, shingles, windows, and doors. Many of us equate the personal experience of 'home' with the physical 'house'. The ability to separate the house (the physical asset) from the home (the personal experiences) makes it possible for you to begin viewing your house as a tool for developing and managing wealth.

Homeowners and new home buyers who can learn to separate in their minds the home (emotional) from the house (logical) are the ones who will best be able to integrate their real estate into their overall short and long-term financial goals. After all, the real goal is to build wealth and financial safety moving forward for yourself and your family.

#40 - How Should You Repay Your Mortgage?

The answer to this question is unique to every individual who is planning to buy or already owns a home. Some of the factors at play are your current cash flow, how you get paid at work, job security, what other financial goals and obligations you have, and ultimately your long-term goals with the house.

As a homeowner, this can lead to a few different questions:

- Do I repay my new loan over 30 years or 15 years?
- Do I make extra payments each month to pay the mortgage down faster?
- Do I pay just the minimum payment so I can put my extra money in savings or pay off other debts?

If you have plenty of extra cash left over at the end of each month, and all of your other "buckets" are full or being adequately filled (see How to Prioritize Your Cash Flow on page ___), then paying extra on your mortgage, or even choosing a shorter-term mortgage may make sense for you, such as a 10, 15, 20, or even a 25-year mortgage.

On the other hand, if you do not yet have sufficient cash reserves set aside for those unexpected cash needs, it typically doesn't make sense to pay back your mortgage faster. Likewise, if you have other higher-interest, non-tax deductible debts, your extra cash flow should go toward paying those off before making extra payments toward your mortgage. In addition, if you have concerns about your job or your income fluctuates throughout the course of the year due to commissions or bonuses, then a 30-year mortgage (meaning, a 30-year repayment plan) most likely is the safest. Besides, you can always pay extra on a 30-year mortgage when able, and then enjoy the minimum payments when times get tougher.

The real key here is to not compartmentalize this decision. Meaning, how you choose to repay your mortgage impacts virtually every other aspect of your finances. When you choose to send an extra $500 each month to your mortgage servicer, remember that that same $500 can never be used for paying off a credit card or investing for your children's college education.

It is natural for many homeowners to start out with the goal of paying down, and off, their mortgage as fast as possible. But when you consider all the factors, this is not always the most prudent financial decision. Make sure all of your other financial needs and goals are in alignment with your mortgage repayment plan so you don't get caught with all of your money IN the house when you most need it.

#41 - The New Location, Location, Location

"We're not lost. We're locationally challenged."
– John M. Ford

When it comes to real estate, the phrase, "location, location, location" always described the importance of where your house was physically located. But these days, "location, location, location" needs to also be applied to your cash and cash flow.

With this in mind, how do you compare the investment in your house to other investments, such as your 401(k), a savings account, stocks or bonds, or even cash in your sock drawer?

Here are six crucial tests to use whenever you are deciding where to put your money:

1. **Safety** *(how safe will my money be? What is the chance of losing my investment?)*
2. **Liquidity** *(how readily available will my money be and how quickly can I get to it if needed?)*
3. **Rate of Return** *(how much interest will I earn by investing here?)*
4. **Taxes** *(do I get some tax savings or benefit from this investment?)*
5. **Leverage** *(how can I invest a small amount of money to control a larger asset?)*
6. **Diversification** *(don't keep all of my eggs in one basket!)*

Whether you are meeting with a financial planner to begin investing for your future, preparing to make a down payment on a new house, or making extra payments toward your debt, these six terms should be understood and applied when it comes to finding the best "location, location, location" for your hard-earned money.

Furthermore, for most homeowners, more of your monthly income will flow through your house than will flow through any other investments. This means how you manage the location of your money when it comes to your house (i.e. down payment, extra principle reductions, home equity, amount borrowed, etc.) is critical in achieving financial safety and abundance.

#42 - Wealth and the House

"Every person who invests in well-selected real estate in a growing section of a prosperous community adopts the surest and safest method of becoming independent, for real estate is the basis of wealth." – Theodore Roosevelt

Your House Wealth

Real estate appreciation has played the greatest role in shaping most American's net worth. As your house value increases over time, and your mortgage gets paid down, the equity in your house grows. So what is "house wealth"? The wealth in a house is its current value minus any liabilities against the house:

House Value – House Liabilities = House Wealth

Many homeowners refer to this simply as "equity in my home". The reason to know call it "house wealth" is that it forces us to consider it as an actual investment. For most of us, our house-related wealth may be our largest single asset. So if this is the case, you must ask yourself, "Am I managing the wealth in my house as carefully as I manage my other investments?"

At its core, a house is meant to meet our physical needs for safety and shelter, as well as our social needs of family and community. But if it stopped there, most of us would live in a very simple rectangular structure with a roof, or possibly even rent a house without the long-term commitment that comes with owning.

Yet, year after year, housing surveys continue to show that American's number one reason for buying and owning a home is the long-term financial investment opportunity that it provides.

The House as a Wealth Creation Tool

Increasingly, the house is a key building block for wealth creation. Many people cite "buying a first house" as the reason they began saving for the first time. But if owning a house can play such a vital role in a person's ability to achieve financial freedom, what should a new buyer know? Or for that matter, how should an existing homeowner learn to better manage the wealth already inside their house?

Critical questions should be asked and researched, to ensure maximum return-on-investment when it comes to buying and owning real estate.

- How much down payment *should* I make to optimize my investment?
- What role does the interest rate really play in obtaining a home loan?
- Should I pay "points" to get a lower interest rate, or keep my fees lower and accept a slightly higher rate?

- Should I wait to save up more money to make a larger down payment or buy as soon as I am financially able to?

Owning a house provides an incredible path to build wealth over time. Just remember, the wealth IN your house must be viewed and treated like other investments would be.

#43 - The 3-Legged Stool

The "3-Legged Stool" is a crucial thinking and planning tool for making smart borrowing and repayment decisions when it comes to buying and owning a home.

The three "legs" are: Liquidity, Safety, and Rate of Return. These are the three key filters for making all investment decisions, whether it's what to do with $100 left over at the end of the month, where your retirement savings get invested or deciding between 10% versus 20% down payment to buy that new house.

Let's start with liquidity. This means, how easily accessible is my money when I put it somewhere? We all understand that money in a savings or checking account is extremely "liquid", meaning I could drive to the closest ATM machine and get some of it within minutes. Money in a retirement account, on the other hand, is a bit harder to get to, thus there is less "liquidity". But how about money used for the down payment on a house? How easy is it to get some of that money back out should you ever absolutely need it? The short answer is, there are only two ways to access home equity – sell or borrow. Borrowing can be in the form of a refinance or taking out a home equity loan or line of credit. Either of these options can take anywhere from two weeks up to two months, depending on your situation and the market. Thus, it is critical for home buyers and homeowners to understand that equity in a home has the least amount of liquidity when compared to other investments. So be smart when deciding how much to put down or if you decide to pay extra each month toward your mortgage payment.

Now, on to safety. The second "leg" of the stool refers to, *"How likely will my money be there when I need it?"* How safe is the equity in your home compared to other investments? Equity is defined as the difference between how much you owe (mortgage) and how much your house is worth (purchase price). While there are a number of ways you can lose the equity in your home (depreciation, foreclosure, etc.), the short answer is that home equity is considered pretty safe relative to other places you could "store" your money. It could be compared to putting money into a long-term bond...not easily accessible but relatively safe.

Finally, the rate of return must be considered. *"How much interest will I earn by putting my money somewhere?"* While stocks tend to be considered riskier investments, people balance that risk with the likelihood of a better rate of return over time. On the other hand, your checking or savings account offers a very low rate of return but is extremely safe and liquid. But what rate of return does the equity in your home provide? To keep this lesson brief, the answer is zero rate of return. Yes, the actual equity in your home earns zero rate of return.

By paying down a mortgage faster, or making a larger down payment, you do indeed SAVE interest. And when your home value increases, thus increasing the amount of equity you have, there is a feeling that your equity is making some rate of return. But the rate of return is on your house, not directly on the money you put INTO the house.

#44 - The Only Way You Make Money Owning Real Estate

This is one of the most powerful lessons I have ever received throughout my real estate career. This lesson changed the way I approach the financing of my own houses, as well as the advice I have given to clients over the years to help them make smarter borrowing decisions.

There are two ways to create and build, wealth IN your house. By wealth IN your house, I mean home equity...the difference between what your house is worth and what you owe in mortgages on it:

1. **Down payment, and the ensuing pay down of your mortgage over time.**
2. **Appreciation.**

(Yes, for some there is a third way, sometimes called "sweat equity" that I'm leaving out as it is too difficult to put a value on it. If you fix up your house, remodel your kitchen, add on a new room, put a new roof on, or mow the lawn extra well...all that might add value and it might not. So for simplicity sake, this lesson will focus on the two ways above that impact virtually everyone.)

In looking at the two ways above to create wealth in your house, I want you to notice the key differentiator. One is determined by YOU (down payment; mortgage pay down), and the other is determined by THE MARKET (appreciation).

Example #1: Let us assume you bought a $200,000 house and put $50,000 down when you first bought your home. Along the way, you have paid down your mortgage balance by $10,000 as a result of your normal monthly mortgage payments. Now, let's assume it's been a few years and you are ready to sell, but lo and behold, your house is worth the exact same amount as when you bought it. **Did you make any money?**

Ignoring the typical costs that go along with selling a house, you would walk away with $60,000 from your sale. This is the same $60,000 you put into the house yourself.

Sticking with the above example, what if you had put $100,000 down originally, and paid an extra $100 extra each month toward your mortgage, paying your mortgage balance down by an additional $3,600 over the last three years? In this case (and still ignoring fees, etc.) you would walk away with $103,600. Again I ask, **did you make any money?** It sure feels like you did, when you look at that $103,600 in your bank account now. But...wasn't that already your money to begin with?

Example #2: Using the same assumptions as above, your $200,000 house you purchased with $50,000 down three years ago, is now worth $250,000 thanks to a great real estate market driving up your house value. Again you paid down your mortgage by $10,000 since buying your house. This time when you sell, you walk away with the $60,000 you've put into it along with the $50,000 the market added in appreciation, for a grand total of $110,000. Did you make money? If so, what is your profit?

Drum roll please...your profit is $50,000 (minus any costs associated with selling). Yep, when selling your house it's easy to be excited about this huge chunk of proceeds coming your way. But the reality is, the only money you really made on the house is the $50,000 the market provided you. Remember, $50,000 of the $110,000 was your initial down payment...already your asset. The final $10,000 in proceeds was already your money that went toward paying down your mortgage each month.

Still not convinced there is only one way most of us really make money by owning real estate?

Example #3: Imagine you put $0 down on that $200,000 house, and never paid down a penny of principle on your mortgage balance for three years (i.e. an interest-only loan). Your house is now worth $250,000 thanks to the market, and you owe $200,000 – the same amount as when you bought it. Again ignoring the costs of selling, you walk away with $50,000 of profit.

The point of this lesson is this: Don't be confused by how you make money owning a house. A larger down payment doesn't make you more money. Paying extra on your mortgage each month doesn't increase your profits. Financing with a 15-year mortgage instead of a 30-year mortgage doesn't necessarily increase your rate of return investing in a house.

Are there other factors that must be considered? Absolutely! Interest rates, cash flow, potential tax deductions just to name a few. But by understanding that sinking all of your available cash, and extra money each month, into paying down your mortgage, doesn't necessarily increase your profit as a homeowner, you can make much smarter decisions from here on out!

#45 - How Liquid Is Your Home Equity?

When learning how to apply financial planning concepts to the world of real estate and mortgages, there can be a bit of a learning curve. But once grasped, a homeowner can feel extremely empowered and confident in the decisions they make when borrowing and repaying mortgage debt throughout their life.

One of the most important financial planning concepts a homeowner can understand is "liquidity". Liquidity, along with safety and rate of return, makes up the "3-Legged Stool" you should use as an important filter when deciding where to locate your hard-earned money.

Liquidity, in this case, refers to how readily available your money, or an asset, is. Cash under your mattress is extremely liquid. Checking accounts and even most investments are available the same day or within 24 hours if you suddenly need money. Getting money out of your 401(k) would be a little tougher. So how easy is it to access the "wealth" inside your house, called home equity?

With this in mind, we must realize that home equity is an investment. Home equity is simply the difference between what your house is worth and what you currently owe in the way of a mortgage. Home equity is the result of your initial down payment when you purchased your home, plus the additional principal payments you have made each month, in addition to any increased value your house enjoys due to the market. Most likely, the amount of equity in your home grows as a combination of all three elements.

The mistake most homeowners make it not treating home equity like any other investments. They make large down payments whenever possible; sometimes even paying cash for a new house. They send in extra money every month beyond the minimum monthly payment. They choose a 15-year mortgage over a 30-year mortgage, with the goal to pay down the loan faster and in theory, minimize long-term interest expense.

None of these decisions are necessarily right or wrong. But what is the best option for you? Well, ...it depends.

The reality is, there are only two ways to access the equity inside of your house:

1. Sell (typically taking 30-60+ days)
2. Borrow (with a refinance or a home equity line of credit, taking 15-45 days)

As you can quickly see, neither option is going to provide you the much-needed money if an emergency was to come up or even an investment opportunity was to presents itself.

So what is the best solution? Again, it depends. There is no one-size-fits-all plan. For many, having money in the bank, that is easily accessible when needed, puts helps us sleep better at night. Yet, at the same time, most of those same people have the majority of their money stored in their home in the form of "home equity", and are choosing to pay extra on their mortgage every month versus investing those same dollars in a more liquid place.

Thus, the best solution is to be educated on what liquidity means and how important it is to have easy, quick access to your money when and if necessary.

Home equity is not liquid when compared to other options for storing your hard earned cash. So plan wisely when deciding how much to put down on your next house, and how much to send in each month with your mortgage payment.

#46 - An Introduction to Liability Management for Homeowners

Welcome to homeownership! Now the real (and fun) work begins.

Most people, especially those working closely with a financial advisor, are familiar with the phrase "asset management". This is the process, and idea, of managing your assets. These might include everything from your retirement accounts and investments to your wills or trusts, clear down to your savings in a money market.

But who is helping you manage the other side of your balance sheet? That would be your liabilities. I learned long ago that the fastest way to help you increase your net worth, and enjoy more assets in need managing, was to teach you how to manage your liabilities.

Liabilities refer to all of your debts, or anyone you owe money to. For most people, this includes credit cards, student loans, auto loans, boat loans and the biggest one of all, your mortgage. Add in the fact that all of your liabilities come with different interest rates and various repayment terms. Some have interest rates that change periodically, and some are fixed forever. Some are revolving, like credit cards, and some are on a set repayment plan over a set number of years (autos, mortgages, etc.) Some, like your mortgage and even a home equity loan, may provide tax deductions.

Thus, liability management is learning how to best manage all of these various debts with the primary goals being to:

- Maximize your monthly cash flow and ability to save
- Have a plan to eliminate all "bad" debt
- Constantly minimize your overall cost of borrowing amongst all of your debts (not just your mortgage)
- Take full advantage of any tax benefits certain liabilities provide
- Grow your net worth (and as a result, your financial safety and freedom)

What is "bad debt," you ask? Bad debt, by my definition, refers to any of your liabilities that provide no tax benefits and are not secured by an asset that goes up in value. Yes, you guessed it...that pretty much leaves the mortgage for most people as the only "good" debt by this definition.

Liability Management means taking a holistic view when looking at all of your liabilities. Keep in mind the real money game of life that we should all be playing is 'net worth'. Being debt free, or earning lots of money, or having low-interest rates, are all "sub" games of the real game – net worth. Net worth is the difference between your assets and liabilities. So, to increase your net worth you can either save more or pay down your liabilities.

It is said that what gets measured, improves. Putting this wisdom into action, I encourage you to calculate your Net Worth monthly, or at least quarterly. Do it on paper, or use a simple spreadsheet and list all of your assets on one side (estimated value of your house, cars, savings, and investments, etc.) and total them up. On the other side of your paper, or the next column over in Excel, list all of your liabilities (mortgage, home equity loan, auto loans, student loans, credit cards, etc.). Make it your goal to grow your net worth over time.

Learning to manage your liabilities will be the quickest and most effective path for you to increase savings, build wealth, and enjoy financial peace of mind.

#47 - How to Protect Your Home Equity

Home equity is the difference between what your house is worth and what you owe on it. If you are like many people across the country, the amount of equity in your home surpasses all other investments combined!

Assume you purchased a $400,000 house three years ago, with 10% down payment, or $40,000. After paying the mortgage down the last few years, let's assume you currently owe about $350,000. Let's also say your house has appreciated (increased in value) by an average of 5% each year, meaning your house is currently valued at $463,000. Using round numbers, you have $113,000 of home equity or as I like to call it, House Wealth. Feels pretty good, right?

With this in mind, how are you protecting it? Meaning, what measures have you put in place to make sure you don't lose any, or all, of that $113,000 in the above example?

To determine this, you must first understand the threats that exist. Depreciation is a big one. This is when the market value begins going down, thus eroding the value of your house, and as a result, the amount of home equity you have.

Another big threat most homeowners never imagine facing is foreclosure. The reality is, you could pay your monthly mortgage payment on time for years, but suddenly find yourself in a financial situation where you are unable to make your payments for a month or more. This could be from a loss of job, a medical crisis, or any other financial catastrophe you weren't prepared for. Only too late do you learn that the typical rule mortgage servicing companies follow is that after three missed payments, the foreclosure process begins!

There are other threats too, but let's shift to answering the question of how to protect yourself and the home equity you are enjoying.

1. **Cash Reserves** – this is the easiest and the first, place to start. If you have any fear of a job loss or other financial obstacles ahead, sock more money into savings. Remember, the banks don't care how long you've been paying them back...they only care how you are paying them now, and going forward. Having plenty of cash on hand protects your ability to make your mortgage payments when unexpected events arise.

2. **Home Equity Line of Credit** – If you can, I always recommend having a home equity line of credit (HELOC) in place on your home. It transforms your home equity into a more accessible, liquid asset. If you run out of cash and don't want to tap into your retirement accounts early, a HELOC gives you easy, quick access to money IN your house when most needed. Even if you plan to never use it, having

one in place "just in case" is a great protection tool.

3. **Affordable Payment** – this may seem obvious, but just remember this rule of thumb: you can always pay extra on a 30-year mortgage to pay it off faster when times are good, and make the minimum payments when times are tough. Choosing a 15-year mortgage, or any other shorter-term mortgage that comes with a larger monthly payment removes this flexibility for most.

I'm leaving out the fact that there is insurance you can buy to protect you in the event of losing a job to ensure your mortgage payments get paid. I am not for or against these, and other ways. My goal here is to keep the focus on the protection strategies YOU can control, and that are easiest to put in place.

#48 - Should You Pay Off Your Mortgage Faster?

For nearly two decades now, I have seen too many homeowners paying extra toward their mortgage without first having sufficient cash in the bank to weather unforeseen financial problems or while carrying other high-interest consumer debt. Do you fall into this category? The hard truth is this: most homeowners should be using their extra money for other important purposes before sending in those additional dollars to pay down their mortgage balance ahead of schedule.

If you are wondering whether or not it makes good financial sense for YOU and your family to pay extra on your monthly mortgage payment, here is an extremely helpful formula I have taught to thousands of homeowners over the years of consulting and advising. Whether you have $50, $500, or $5,000 left over at the end of your month, here are the "buckets" to put your money in, and the order in which to do so that we teach:

1. **Establish Cash Reserves:** Set a goal for how much you and your family need for all of the "what ifs" that may come your way. This isn't a new idea, but unfortunately just about every financial study done shows that most people couldn't last 2 months without their

income. I call this your "sleep well at night" money. Whether it's a fixed amount, like $10,000, or a specific number of months of expenses, set the goal and start filling this bucket before your extra money goes anywhere else.

2. **Eliminate Consumer Debt:** Once you have achieved your Cash Reserves goal, start attacking any and all non-mortgage debt you have. Pay off those auto loans, credit cards, and even student loans. I don't care how low the interest rate is. The problem is the monthly payments. Since we live lives of cash flow, the monthly payments to "bad debt" are sucking up your hard-earned take-home pay instead of helping you build your future.

3. **Build Savings and Liquidity:** With your "sleep well at night" bucket filled, and your consumer debt paid off, it is now time to accelerate your efforts in building your net worth and long-term financial safety. This means, in addition to any retirement contributions you are making regularly, either on your own or through your employer, you must begin saving money for all of those short, mid-, and other long-term goals you have. These might include college savings, setting aside cash for next year's vacations, and money invested with a trusted financial planner that gives you flexibility down the

road for possible career changes, loss of jobs, or larger unexpected financial problems. *(If you are wondering how much to save here, my advice is...as much as you possibly can! But if you are like me and want a more specific goal, shoot for one year of your income saved in these various "buckets" that don't include retirement accounts or your Cash Reserves.)*

4. **Pay Off House:** Your goal should absolutely be to someday own a house with no mortgage and no longer have a mortgage payment. But too often I see homeowners jumping to this step before the first three, mostly due to poor advice or emotional reasons. The key is, make sure this goal applies to your FINAL house. Meaning, is the house you are currently living in the same house you imagine being retired in and enjoying no mortgage payments in? If not, consider continuing to fill up the first three "buckets" and increasing your net worth in a much more liquid and productive way.

#49 - Personal Debt vs. Investment Debt

Personal Debt

In America, we are all too familiar with personal debt. This refers to the money we borrow to purchase items (assets) that will most likely go down in value (depreciate) over time. It is the most costly type of debt a person can have because eventually, the item purchased will depreciate to $0. Something you purchased five or ten years ago for $50-$100 finds itself front and center at your next garage sale for $5 or worse yet...being donated to the local Goodwill just to clear space for more "stuff".

- **The dreaded auto loan:** Talk about investing in an asset that depreciates seemingly by the day! Imagine borrowing $30,000 for that new car, with an interest rate of 6%. Your monthly payment of $580 over five years will pay back the $30,000 you borrowed, along with $4,799 of interest expense. At the end of five years, you might find yourself with a car now worth $10,000. Your payments of $34,799 ($30,000 original cost plus $4,799 of interest paid) over the last five years, minus the current value of $10,000, means

the net loss of this investment was
$24,799.

Other common types of personal debt include
most credit card purchases, personal loans, boat
loans, and pretty much any unsecured type of
debt.

Investment Debt

On the other hand, investment debt refers to
money borrowed to purchase something that
will typically increase in value (appreciate) over
time. While this is a form of debt, it often helps
increase a person's net worth. Unlike personal
debt, ***investment debt*** is often secured by the
asset being borrowed against.

- **A home mortgage:** One of the most
  common types of investment debt is
  a mortgage used to purchase
  residential real estate. Consider the
  purchase of a $200,000 house with
  $160,000 mortgage borrowed over
  30 years with a 7% interest rate. If
  the house itself were to appreciate at
  4% per year, it would be worth
  $662,700 in 30 years. The interest
  you pay over that time would total
  $223,214. Thus, your initial cost of
  the house ($200,000) plus the
  interest expense ($223,214) would
  total $423,214. However, you would
  now own a house worth $662,700,
  resulting in a gain of $239,486 of

increased net worth! *(Yes, there are lots of variables I am leaving out to get across the point, but they are also left out of the personal debt discussion above.)*

So what is the point? There are a few key lessons I want you to get from this way of thinking:

1. How you borrow, and what types of debt you carry, impacts every aspect of your financial future.
2. This is where the idea of "good debt" and "bad debt" come in to play.
3. You may be like so many others where you grow up believing all debt is bad debt, but that's not necessarily the case.
4. Ideally, work toward having ONLY investment debt...debt that is allowing you to secure a financial asset that has the capability of improving your net worth over time.

#50 - Your Mortgage and Retirement

Imagine ten, fifteen, or even 20 years from now. You are just coming down from the excitement of your pre-retirement party. Your co-workers, friends, and family have left. The helium balloons are hovering half-way between the floor and ceiling, while confetti and silly string create a nightmare for the cleaning crew.

Then it hits you. In a few short months, you will be on a fixed retirement income. Yet, you still have ten or fifteen years left on your 30-year mortgage. Years ago when you obtained this mortgage, you had a hazy goal of having no mortgage when you retired.

Now, you're scrambling with your financial planner to determine how long your retirement "nest egg" will last since you must withdraw more each month than originally planned due to the still-existing mortgage payment.

How does this happen? Simple. ***Your mortgage and your mortgage repayment plan wasn't a key part of your retirement planning.***

So the questions you now have are:

- Should I refinance my mortgage to a shorter term that matches my retirement age goal?
- Do I figure out how much extra to pay each month to ensure my

current mortgage is paid off in time for retirement?

- Is using my extra cash flow to pay down my mortgage the best financial decision in the long-run?
- Should I ramp up my investing and savings to then be able to pay off the mortgage all at once when I retire?
- What about some of my other debts like the auto loan, or student loans, or that credit card balance for last year's vacation?
- How does this mortgage repayment impact the rest of my financial goals, such as saving for college and retirement?

These questions all center on what I call *Liability Management*. Years ago I came to the realization that while financial planners around the country were focused on managing assets for their clients, and mapping out a path to retirement, nobody was truly helping people manage the other side of the balance sheet...the liabilities. And the truth is, how we manage our monthly cash flow, and the choices we make throughout a lifetime of borrowing and repayment of debts plays a critical role in your ability to retire *when* you want and *how* you want. Through better management and planning on the mortgage and liability side, you can be debt free sooner and increase your net worth faster and easier.

Review your mortgage and any other debts you have with a trusted mortgage professional as well as your financial advisor. Together, make sure you are optimized with regards to minimizing your cost of borrowing, maximizing your tax benefits, and on the right track to be mortgage free when you choose to be mortgage free.

#51 - Five Reasons You Might Want to Consider Refinancing

Owning a home and building equity opens up many opportunities. As a homeowner, there will be times you wonder if refinancing your mortgage makes sense. Rightly so, as there are quite a few reasons getting a new mortgage can improve your financial future if done right. Here are some of the most common (and less common) reasons you might want to consider refinancing your mortgage at some point.

Word of Caution from the author: Always remember, there are costs involved when refinancing, and it is a big financial decision. So don't rush into it, and be sure you work with an expert who can educate you and talk you through the pros AND the cons of refinancing. Don't make short-term decisions that negatively impact your long-term goals. And do NOT waste your savings after you do refinance! Ok, back to the five reasons:

1. **Take advantage of lower interest rates:**

   - This is the most obvious, and the most common, reason homeowners look to refinance their existing mortgage. If interest rates have dropped since you first bought your house, you may be able to take advantage and lower your monthly payment by refinancing and getting a new mortgage. This can provide a quick boost to the ability to save or pay off other debts faster. Just be careful you don't simply spend your savings.

2. **Get cash out:**

    *   If you are considering a remodel, or perhaps would like to consolidate some higher interest debt, or need cash for an opportunity that has come along, you may consider looking into a cash-out refinance. There are limitations, but simply put, you may be able to access some of the equity in your home to achieve the above goals. Often borrowing against your home is less expensive than other options. Your house is NOT an ATM machine, but done strategically, safely, and within an overall plan, your house can be a valuable financial tool.

3. **Get rid of mortgage insurance:**

    *   If you bought your house with less than 20% down payment, it's likely you have monthly mortgage insurance included in your payment. As you pay your mortgage balance down, and your house appreciates in value to the point you have 20% or more equity, you may have the opportunity to refinance and get a new mortgage without mortgage insurance. Keep in

mind you MIGHT be able to accomplish this goal directly through your mortgage servicing company, but if not, refinancing can be a good option.

4. **Consolidate a 1st and 2nd mortgage:**

- Another strategic way you may have financed your house with less than 20% down was by doing a first mortgage to 80% loan-to-value, and then borrowing the difference between this and your down payment in the form of a second mortgage or home equity loan. This is often done as an alternative to dealing with mortgage insurance (see #3). Or perhaps you took out a home equity loan or line of credit to remodel your house. If interest rates are favorable, and you have sufficient equity for it to make sense, refinancing to consolidate your first and second mortgages into one new mortgage can make good financial sense.

5. **Change your mortgage terms:**

- Perhaps you were overly aggressive or just had a fear of debt, leading you to finance your house using a 15-year mortgage. If you find that these higher than normal monthly payments are impeding your ability to save elsewhere, avoid using credit cards for vacations, or even worse, not allowing you to maximize your retirement contributions, you may want to consider refinancing to a longer-term mortgage. Even if a 30-year fixed-rate mortgage comes with a slightly higher interest rate, the lower required payments can free up cash flow to achieve other important financial goals. On the other hand, maybe you hope to retire in ten years, yet you have 22 years left on your current mortgage. If cash flow is good, and your other debts are all paid off, refinancing to a shorter term mortgage might make sense. Again, this assumes all of your other financial "ducks" are in a row.

#52 - 3 Questions to Help You Decide if Refinancing Makes Sense

Just about everyone who owns a home, and has a mortgage, will consider the possibility of refinancing the existing mortgage at some point. This occurs for a variety of reasons. Perhaps interest rates have dropped and an opportunity to borrow the same amount of money at a lower cost has become available. Maybe you are considering a remodel and are interested in using some of your 'house wealth', or home equity, to pay for it rather than dipping into savings. You might wish to consolidate some other debts or get rid of mortgage insurance. Or you would like to explore shortening the term of your mortgage so better match with your retirement goals or simply be debt-free sooner.

So how do you truly determine if a refinance makes SMART financial sense for you?

Here are 3 critical questions to consider before you move forward (or do not) on a refinance.

1. **What are your key objectives with the refinance?** Are you trying to save money for other things, pay off your mortgage faster, or consolidate other debt? Understanding your most important goals you hope to achieve through a refinance is important. If you are trying to reduce your payment and take advantage of lower rates, what are the costs involved?

And do the short and long-term objectives of the refinance outweigh the costs involved? Imagine saving $100 per month from refinancing, and then applying it back toward your new mortgage at the newly acquired lower rate (also called a same-pay refinancing). What if that allows you to pay the mortgage off many years sooner? What if you save that $100 in a college fund for your 3-year old child, earning interest for the next 15 years? What if you are suddenly able to pay off other high-interest credit cards twice as fast using the monthly savings from a refinance, freeing up even more money each month?

2. **How long do you expect to have this mortgage?** This is an important consideration due to the fact there are always costs involved with refinancing, and you must calculate your break-even analysis when refinancing. For example, let's say the costs of refinancing add up to $3,500, and your potential savings will be $100 per month. By dividing $3,500 by the $100, you realize your break-even is 35 months. This simple math now tells you that as long as you'll be your house, or keep this mortgage, for three years, it makes sense to move forward.

Keep in mind, other factors do come into play, such as typically a month off from making a payment after closing your refinance. So what you do with those dollars should be factored in. Imagine having no payment for a month and using those dollars to pay off a high-interest credit card in one fell swoop that was costing you another $100 per month. In addition, what good will you do with the $100 per month you are now enjoying due to the lower mortgage payment? When considering all the factors involved, it can be surprising how quickly a homeowner can actually recoup the costs of refinancing and dramatically shorten the break-even time.

3. **What other loan options or rate/fee scenarios might make sense?** There are many ways to structure a refinance, and the associated costs involved. Misunderstood by many homeowners are the options available to them on how to structure the rate and fees to best meet their short and long-term goals. You might look into reducing the fees, even clear down to zero, by accepting a slightly higher interest rate. This creates a much faster break-even point. Going the other direction, if you have a specific monthly payment target, you may choose to pay extra to get an even lower rate than initially suggested. Sometimes looking into reducing your 30-year mortgage down to a 15-year, 20-year, or even a 25-year mortgage can make sense or

increase the overall benefit of a refinance initially designed for other purposes.

It is all about creating a better financial future

In the end, whether or not you refinancing makes sense should really boil down to this: will it put me in a better financial position down the road? Will refinancing help you achieve your overall short and long-term financial goals faster or easier? These three questions, and a thorough analysis of your current situation and goals can all be determined fairly quickly by a top-notch mortgage professional who has the right tools and understanding of your goals.

49723719R00087

Made in the USA
Columbia, SC
27 January 2019